# JOHN JOE McGINLEY

# FAMINE, MURDER AND EVICTION

## THE HISTORY OF A RURAL PARISH

GLASSAGH PUBLISHING
Printing Your Dreams .

Published in 2023 by Glassagh Publishing Glassagh, Derrybeg, Letterkenny, County Donegal, Republic of Ireland

Telephone: 00353 83 1818 437
Email: info@glassaghpublishing.ie
Web: www.glassaghpublishing.ie

While every effort has been made to ensure the accuracy of all information contained in this book, neither the author nor the publisher accepts liability for any errors or omissions made.

Book design by Joe Coyle Media & Design,
joecoyledesign@gmail.com

# CONTENTS

*This book is dedicated to my father John Mór McGinley. A man who left Ireland as a young man but whose heart was always in Donegal. He taught me that no matter where we wander our home is always in Gweedore.*

*Rest in peace, Dad.*

# INTRODUCTION

I was born in Edinburgh, but my DNA is 100% Gweedore. My mother was born and raised in Brinalack and my father along the winding road in Glasserchoo.

Whilst being raised by emigrant parents in Scotland, every summer we would come home to Donegal.

As soon as the schools shut, we would leave Edinburgh usually in the back of my father's work transit van, six kids and suitcases sitting in the back, no seat belts then. We would head for the Gorbals where a convoy of buses – Feda, McGinley, and Collins – would be waiting to take mothers and children to the ferry to cross to Ireland. Children, cases and even bikes would pile aboard heading for Stranraer or Cairnryan.

The most exciting part of the journey was exploring the boat while mothers – who were born so close to each other but who were now living with their husbands in

Glasgow, Edinburgh and beyond – caught up with each other and exchanged gossip of the months gone by.

We ran excitedly on deck and watched Scotland fade into the distance as Ireland came into view.

Then it was back on to the buses waiting for us on the other side to take us to the many rural parishes of Donegal. Our bus was heading home to Gweedore but we'd have two stops on our journey, Dungiven in the shadow of the RUC station for tea and then Letterkenny where toys for the summer would be purchased. Many a cowboy gun, bow and arrow or tea set was purchased in the Square before we set off on our final leg home.

As we approached Gweedore the bus would stop at lanes and small white cottages where tearful grandparents embraced their children and grandchildren they had not seen since last summer or the last family funeral. My grandfather's home was down a winding lane and as we approached it, we would be apprehensive as young children can be, but this would soon fade as he helped unpack our suitcases and we raced around the house to fields that would now become our playground for the next few months.

It was in these years of summer that my love for Gweedore grew and when I finally returned to the parish permanently in 2014, I decided I wanted to give something back to my new home. I created a website *www.wildatlanticgweedore* and a social media suite which included a Twitter account *@Gweedore_WAWay* and Facebook page Wild Atlantic Gweedore. All designed to showcase the beauty, history and people of Gweedore to the world. Part of the project was to collate as many tales as possible of history and folklore from the parish and surrounding areas. I have decided to amalgamate these blogs into this book, *Famine, Murder and Eviction*.

I have been interested in the stories of Gweedore ever since my grandfather would tell me of the tales of the parish as we sat on long summer evenings looking out to Inishirrer.

It is this man – Jack Ferry – who told me of the sinking of HMS Wasp and of Black Jack Adair and Lord George Hill.

He not only put up with screaming grandchildren for summer after summer, he inspired me to write these stories and to him, I would like to say thank you.

I hope you enjoy these tales from the rural parish of Gweedore and don't forget to follow me on Twitter and Facebook.

# CHAPTER 1
# GAOTH DOBHAIR—THE AQUEOUS ESTUARY

There are about 2,500 civil parishes in Ireland. Each contains an average of 24 townlands, and each of these parishes has its history, folklore and legends.

I want to share with you tales from one rural parish which has seen evictions, murder and rebellion and witnessed events which have been pivotal to Irish history. A small but beautiful area in Donegal called Gweedore or Gaoth Dobhair in Irish.

Gweedore is the anglicisation of the original and official Irish name Gaoth Dobhair. Gaoth refers to an inlet of the sea at the mouth of the Crolly River, known as An Ghaoth. It is the boundary between Gweedore to the north and The Rosses to the south. Dobhar is an old Irish word for water. Therefore, Gaoth Dobhair translates as "the aqueous estuary".

The name Gweedore or Gaoth Dobhair refers to the Catholic parish of the same name, not to any one village or town. The villages of Bunbeg, Derrybeg, Glassagh, Brinalack, Dunlewey and others are collectively known as Gweedore.

Situated along the Wild Atlantic way Gaoth Dobhair stretches some 16 miles (26 km) from Meenaclady in the north to Crolly in the south and around nine miles (14km) from Dunlewey in the east to Magheraclogher in the west. With a population of around 4,000, it is the largest Irish speaking parish in Ireland.

Gaoth Dobhair is known as a bastion of Irish music, language and culture and home to legendary bands such as Clannad and Altan. This combined with its spectacular and haunting scenery and wide wind-swept beaches makes it one of the most picturesque and culturally vibrant places in Ireland and it's up against some pretty strong competition!

With the Atlantic Ocean at its west and the Derryveagh mountains to the east, in 1,500 years, Gweedore has seen pirates, pagans, patriots and even a priest charged with murder.

My book charts the most important historical events and folklore that have shaped not only Gweedore, but which have had ramifications across the world. The parish has seen events that have been pivotal to Irish history but also to the story of America, the United

Kingdom and Australia. Events that have shocked the world, shook the political establishment, and led to social and political change. Such as:

- Canon James McFadden – The land league campaigner and parish priest who was accused of the murder of RIC Inspector William Martin.
- Blackjack Adair and the Derryveagh evictions - It is often said that everyone is well thought off when they die, but there is one man with links to Gweedore of whom that can never be said. He was the Landlord 'Black' Jack Adair, the mastermind of the infamous Derryveagh Evictions.
- The largest medieval stone cross in Ireland lies in the townland of Ray just outside the town of Falcarragh. Standing in the ruins of the Church of Ray, the cross has an ancient history and has witnessed saints and slaughter.
- Lord George Hill the landlord who married not one but two nieces of Jane Austen
- The last battle of the United Irishman-led rebellion of 1798 was not fought, by Irishmen or even on an Irish battlefield, but at sea, off the stormy waters along the Donegal coast in a naval engagement between the French and

British navies. History records this as the battle of Tory Island.

- In 1884 HMS Wasp set out to evict tenant farmers from Inishtrahull but sank on route off the coast of Tory Island was it negligence, sabotage or even a curse?
- Vincent 'Mad Dog' Coll was the Gangster from Gweedore and one of the most notorious Irish American gangsters.
- One of the most haunted places in the commonwealth of Pennsylvania is the scene of a terrible murder of a heavily pregnant Irish emigrant and her brother at the hands of hired killers. The Wiggans patch massacre involved the slaying of Gweedore natives during the mine owners war against the Molly Maguire's.
- Patrick O'Donnell was executed on the 17th of December 1883. The Irish patriot had avenged the Invincible's, hung for the Phoenix Park murders, which rocked the British establishment in Ireland and played a part in delaying home rule.
- The story of Glenveagh Castle built after the Derryveagh evictions, visited by the rich and famous and one owner who may have faked his own death to live a bohemian life in Paris.

- James Duffy, the Gweedore man who won the Victoria cross and was kidnapped by the IRA.
- How the rural electrification programme brought electricity to Gweedore.

And much, much more.

I hope you enjoy these tales from a rural parish and thank you for reading this book.

# CHAPTER 2
# THE FIGHTING PRIEST OF GWEEDORE

Canon James McFadden was a man of deep faith who fought for the rights of his parishioners against unjust foreign landlords. Also known as the 'fighting priest of Gweedore' he was a key member of the Land league, Educator, Parish Priest and a man who was tried for the murder of RIC inspector William Martin.

## THE MAKING OF A PRIEST AND PROTESTER

James McFadden was born in December 1842 to hard working farming stock in Dunmore Carrigart. He had four siblings: John, Michael, Margaret and Grace.

His brother Michael would eventually immigrate to America where he became a rather eccentric Fire inspector in Tennessee, famous for his daily patrols on his trusted steed 'Maggie'. No doubt named after his sister, back in Donegal.(1)

Margaret married in Donegal while Grace would emigrate to Australia but later return to become the future Canon McFadden's housekeeper.

His brother John also found a vocation and spent his life as Brother Norbert McFadden, a member of the Congregation of the Passion of Jesus Christ. An international Catholic religious order also know as the Passionists.

Whilst from a relatively prosperous background, the young James lived through the traumatic years of the famine. The tales he was told growing up of the devastation laid waste in Ireland would have a profound impact on him and instil a burning desire to improve the lives of his fellow Irishmen and women.

He also witnessed the harsh treatment meted out to those that survived the famine by four notorious landlords. Lord George Hill, Lord Leitrim, John Olphert and the most notorious and vicious of the quartet, John George Adair, a wealthy land speculator from county Laois.

John Adair was to incur everlasting infamy throughout Donegal and Ireland by ruthlessly evicting some 244 tenants in the Derryveagh Evictions.

James had a deep faith which would lead to the

priesthood, but he also had a strong sense of injustice and distrust of the landlord system so prevalent in Donegal of the late 1800's.

It would be this faith and his determination to fight this pernicious system that would guide his life.

After studying at the seminary in Maynooth James was ordained on the 1st of January 1871 in St Patricks Cathedral, County Armagh by his uncle the most reverend Dr McGettigan who had recently become the primate of all Ireland.

Father McFadden started his pastoral career as the curate of the parish of Upper Templecrone. He served as a curate in Lettermacward in the Rosses and in Doochary, near Dungloe.

Nearly five years into his priesthood in late 1875, he would move to the parish where he would make history and have such a major impact, that of Gweedore.


## TRAGEDY IN GWEEDORE

James McFadden found the parish of Gweedore struggling to escape the impact of the famine with many tenant farmers just one bad harvest away from starvation and facing the choice between the workhouse or immigration.

He energetically went about trying to improve the conditions of his parishioners.

He obtained many relief grants and used these to build up the local infrastructure.

To ensure as much of the money as possible went to his people, he often acted as unpaid secretary, time-keeper, cashier and even engineer for many of the relief works.

In August 1880 tragedy struck the parish of Gweedore. The 15th of August was feast of the Assumption of Mary and the local church of St Mary's in Gweedore was full of many parishioners standing around the chapel.

On that fateful day, a freak storm broke out and a deluge was thrown from the heavens as thunder rang out. The church was built in a ravine where mass had been said in secret during the penal laws which outlawed the Catholic rites, and a mountain stream ran under the floor of the church.

Soon that stream was overflowing and within minutes of the storm, the water rose up through the floor and the masonry gave way to a deadly torrent that engulfed the worshipers.

The doors became jarred by the rising tide and people began scrambling out of the windows. Water levels inside the church rose to an estimated 12 feet.

Father McFadden, who was aware that fatalities had taken place, began to give general absolution to the congregation and then made his own escape jumping from the altar, smashing a window and making it to safety. Sadly five parishioners died and over 100 were injured.

The youngest who died was 13-year-old altar server Séamus Ó Fearraigh of Stranacorkra, Derrybeg. The others who were drowned were Grace McGarvey, Carrick, Derrybeg, Conal Boyle, Inishmaan Island, and Enrí Ó Gallchobhair and Neil Doherty, both of Magheraclogher, Bunbeg. The Irish Times would describe the flooding as the Gweedore Catastrophe.(2)

To fully understand the tragedy, it is necessary to look at the history of Ireland and Gweedore to see why the Chapel of St Marys was built where it was in a remote ravine over a river and susceptible to flooding.

This unsuitable location of the church ensured that the deluge which engulfed the unfortunate parishioners, whilst a freak event of nature created more damage than was necessary to both parishioners and the building.

The location of the church was because of two things, firstly the restrictive penal laws imposed on Irish Catholics and to a lesser extent Protestant dissenter planters and Quakers to aid the established Church of Ireland and secondly the stubbornness of successive protestant landowners in Gweedore who refused to grant permission for a church to be built on a more suitable site.

Not only did the freak storm damage the Church but

the surrounding countryside was devastated, houses rendered uninhabitable, livestock killed, and crops ruined. An appeal was sent to the British parliament for aid.

£100 was sent on the 18th of August as an initial amount with several members of the government contributing.

The original St Mary's closed in the early 1970's with the opening of a new chapel on higher ground close-by. A memorial stands on the grounds of the old chapel in honour of those who perished in the flood. A mass is offered every year for those that died as Gweedore will never forget the great flood of 1880.

## THE AGITATOR PRIEST

Perhaps aware of his own mortality, McFadden now threw himself into a whirlwind of activity to improve the lives of the people of Gweedore.

A great believer in the power of education he began a program of building schools in the area to ensure even the poorest child had a chance in life.

He also set about campaigning against the prevalence of alcohol abuse which he believed held back the native Irish and was having a detrimental impact on his parishioners.

Prior to McFadden's arrival poteen was made throughout Gweedore and as such he considered drunkenness a scourge, which he was determined to stamp out.

He quickly formed a branch of the Temperance League and set about a campaign of closing down the local "shebeen's" prevalent all across Gweedore.

He would visit these, often chasing out any parishioners he found there. He was also not averse to knocking heads together and smashing them with his trademark blackthorn stick. He was short in stature but strong in will and he soon gained the nickname of 'An Sagart Mor': 'The Big Priest'.(3)

McFadden did not believe the existing system of justice favoured his parishioners, so he set up his own network of district courts. He appointed local people of good standing to act as justices and the decisions of the court soon proved popular.

So popular indeed that the Petty Session court held at Bunbeg every month would convene and immediately adjourn as it had no business to discuss.

Woe betide anyone who would seek a hearing in the British legal system as they would soon find themselves with a boycott placed upon them.(4)

Gweedore was now a hot bed of anti-landlord activity and was even discussed in parliament when in

July 1885 the chief secretary for Ireland Sir William Hart Dyke announced that: "Owing to the disturbed state of the locality it has been found necessary to send four extra constables to Gweedore".(5)

The situation further deteriorated when in 1887 a detachment of soldiers was despatched to Gweedore and stationed in Bunbeg.

In January 1888, at a Land League meeting organised by Michael Davitt the British authorities arranged to have an Irish speaking Royal Irish Constabulary (RIC) Sergeant Owen Mahon from Bunbeg in Gweedore attend to monitor McFadden. When he announced to the crowd in Irish "I am the law in Gweedore" the authorities knew they had to act.(6)

A warrant was issued but McFadden was not in Gweedore but in Armagh where he had gone to celebrate the month's mind Mass of his late uncle Archbishop McGettigan. Undeterred the authorities transferred the warrant to Armagh and expected the local RIC to carry this out.

One local Constable McBride decided he was not a priest hunter and resigned from the force immediately.

Unfortunately, not all the RIC men were as religious as McBride and Father McFadden was soon arrested and transferred to Derry Jail.

As he was led up the steps to the jail McFadden defiantly shouted to the large crowd that had assembled to greet him "Keep the flag flying".

He was accompanied in jail by the MP for Donegal Mr Blaine who was also arrested for a similar offence.

Rioting in support of McFadden soon broke out and the Orange Order mobilised to attack the crowd, aided by a company of Dragoons on horseback.

The authorities fearful of continuing rioting transferred McFadden on the morning of 30th January 1888 to stand trial in Dunfanaghy Donegal.

A large crowd had gathered to see him off, they sang god save Ireland and cheered for McFadden and his fellow prisoner Blaine. The authorities once again fearful of unrest discharged a cannon hoping the noise would create panic and disperse the crowd. It worked to a certain extent as many promptly left, but not to go home, instead they left Derry to accompany McFadden and support him at his trial.

When McFadden appeared in court, he was charged on two counts:

1. Inciting the people to take part in an unlawful conspiracy, to wit, to refuse to pay their rents.
2. Taking part in a criminal conspiracy, namely, the plan of campaign.

Both offences were as a result of his speech at the

Land League event witnessed by Sargent Mahon who was the chief prosecution witness. He gave evidence in court reading out the shorthand notes he had taken as McFadden had spoken.

The second day of the trial had barely begun when a bizarre incident took place. Father Stephens of the nearby townland of Falcarragh a supporter of McFadden was arrested in court charged with coercion. This was a strong sign from the magistrates that McFadden faced a hard task to avoid conviction.

Despite an impassioned closing statement from McFadden's lawyer who extoled the good deeds of the past few years and the fact that he was held in such high regard by his parishioners. The magistrates wanted only one verdict, guilty.

Father McFadden was duly found guilty and sentenced to three months in jail.

He decided to appeal his sentence but was unlucky to come across County court Judge Webb who was vehemently anti Land League and a staunch supporter of the landlord system. Not only was the appeal unsuccessful, but Judge Webb also increased the sentence to six months and ruled out any further right of appeal!

McFadden was finally released on the 16th of October 1888 and his journey from Derry to Gweedore was a great celebration. He was feted by great crowds along the way and given a reception in Letterkenny by the Bishop of Raphoe Dr O'Donnell.

If the authorities believed that Father McFadden would stop his agitation against the landlords, they were mistaken. At a meeting in Magheraclogher in Gweedore on the 19th of December 1888, he gave another rousing speech imploring his parishioners to resist the landlords and join the Land League.

The police note takers were again in attendance and another arrest warrant was issued against McFadden however this would only lead to bloodshed, tragedy and murder.

## THE MURDER OF INSPECTOR WILLIAM MARTIN

Father James McFadden had just been released from Derry jail after serving six months for membership of the Land League and inciting his parishioners to withhold their rents, but his fight against what he perceived as harsh landlord practices and the British system in Ireland was not yet over.

When he became the parish priest of Gweedore in 1875, McFadden encouraged farmers not to pay rent, and rallied his parishioners to challenge alleged improvements of local landlord, Lord George Hill. He was also known to hate heavy drinking and was often seen chasing locals out of Shebeen's with his blackthorn stick.

After another rousing speech in December 1888, the authorities decided that they had sufficient evidence to charge Father McFadden under the Criminal Law and procedures Act 1887.

A summons was issued and served on him on the 15th of January 1889, but he had no intention of attending a court system he did not acknowledge as legitimate or fair.

When he did not appear, a warrant was issued from the court for his arrest.

On the 28th of January, the RIC men went to arrest McFadden, but were denied entry to the parochial house. The following morning, he celebrated mass in St Mary's chapel and returned to his home. A large RIC contingent surrounded his residence, and a standoff was now in play.

That night fires were lit around the parish of Gweedore calling men to defend McFadden. Over 100 assembled, determined to protect their priest.

Father McFadden addressed the crowd from his window, imploring them to go home as he was in no danger. He obviously didn't believe this, as he used the commotion to slip out of his home. He was sheltered by his loyal parishioners as he evaded the RIC over the next few days. Despite the risk of arrest, he refused to abandon his parishioners and returned to St Marys on Sunday the 3rd of February to celebrate mass.

That morning had seen a number of the Royal Irish Constabulary men travel to the chapel to intercept Fr McFadden, who was charged with conspiracy under the Criminal Law and Procedure (Ireland) Act, 1887. That legislation granted greater power to police in relation to agrarian crimes and agitation associated with the Land War. The priest's supposed crime was "conspiracy to induce persons not to pay their rents". He had been served a summons to appear at the Petty Sessions on January 28th – which he ignored.(7)

The RIC surrounded the Chapel and after the mass ended RIC District Inspector William Martin and 42 RIC men attempted to arrest McFadden.

Inspector Martin drew his sword, approached McFadden who was still in his vestments and demanded that he surrender himself into his custody.

The congregation was horrified, seeing a sword drawn on their parish priest and a group of men rushed to his aid. Inspector Martin was soon surrounded and heavily beaten.

Six RIC men went to Inspector Martins aid and a battle began.

The RIC armed with swords and cudgels and the parishioners with granite rocks. One parishioner pulled a paling post and began to beat Inspector Martin about the head, dealing what would prove to be a mortal blow. All the RIC men present received a heavy beating with four seriously injured.

An armed reserve force of police arrived and prepared to fire on the parishioners. They were only stopped by McFadden's pleas and his promise that he would ensure the crowd would disperse and that the parochial house could be used to tend the wounded RIC men.

Inspector Martin was brought into McFadden's study where he died at 2.30pm. A riot had now become a murder and an uproar began as the RIC began arresting those, they felt responsible.

In the confusion, some of the men involved escaped to the surrounding mountains and bogs and managed to avoid the police. Others took flight to Derry and would later sail to America.

The murder sent shock waves all through Ireland. Reporters descended on the area in the aftermath of the death. They were appalled by the remoteness and lack of transport links in Gweedore.

"Bunbeg is at any time a difficult place to reach, it being at the nearest thirty 'long' or Irish miles from civili- sation– that is, civilisation as judged by a railway station."(8)

## THE TRIAL OF FATHER MCFADDEN

At a hearing in Bunbeg, on Monday February 11th, 1889 the charge of conspiracy was formally withdrawn in court, in place of a murder charge against Fr McFadden. Dr Houston, QC, for the priest, criticised the Crown; first, it had brought a "baseless" charge of conspiracy it knew would fail, then dropped it immediately at the sight of a more serious "invented" charge of murder.

"Oh, what a position!" the lawyer exclaimed in court. "I wonder under what inspiration, Press or otherwise, that charge has been trumped up . . ."(9)

McFadden was returned to Derry Jail in a carriage under heavy escort.

The British authorities knew it would be highly unlikely to secure a conviction against a Roman Catholic priest in his native Donegal, so they moved the trial to Portlaoise.

Father McFadden and 35 other men and women were eventually arrested charged with murder and sent to Maryborough Gaol (now Portlaoise Prison).

On the 31st of March, McFadden and 19 of his parishioners were returned for trial at the summer assizes and charged with rioting and the murder of Inspector Martin. This surprised many who had not expected McFadden to be included in those charged with the death of Inspector Martin.

The trial created headlines throughout the world and was even debated in parliament.

On the 4th of April James Stuart the MP for Hoxton raised the arrest of McFadden in the house of Commons. He asked Arthur Balfour Chief Secretary for Ireland:

"I beg to ask the Chief Secretary to the Lord Lieutenant of Ireland whether any evidence, other than police evidence, was brought forward before the magistrates at Letterkenny, connecting Father McFadden, or the other prisoners, committed for trial for the murder of Inspector Martin, with the death of that constable; and whether it is correct, as asserted in the Daily News of Tuesday last, that the statements made by the constables were "made in some instances after the constables had had frequent opportunities of talking over among themselves as to what had happened?"(10)

Thomas Sexton MP, who would later be Lord Mayor of Dublin also raised the matter in the House of Commons on the 12th of April 1889 saying:

"The right hon. Gentleman will not discuss the arrest of Father McFadden. Does he forget the case in which, the Attorney General having declined to proceed against a policeman who was accused on the finding of a coroner's jury of having killed a man at Middleton, the

Chief Baron called attention to the failure of justice, and in the interests of justice the Attorney General was compelled to proceed before a magistrate? It is a question, in the case of Father McFadden, of the exercise of the functions of the Attorney General. What is he about to do? We have a right to know. The materials have been for many days before him; is he going to institute a prosecution or not? The imprisonment of Father McFadden means that the case of the other persons is prejudiced by the closing of the mouth of their principal witness. It means that the accused can make no adequate arrangements for their defence. It means there is no one to look after these poor starving women and children, no one to assist the tenants by endeavouring to promote a settlement with the landlord, should he be willing to come to terms. By your method of arresting Father McFadden, you have done more than, in my memory, has ever been done by any Government to plunge the district into confusion and despair, to bring about breach of the law and peril to life and property. The police were planted about the church from an early hour. The warrant for arrest had been held for several days and no attempt was made to execute it— it was held over while Father McFadden went about the parish on his parochial duties. Why, if, as the Chief Secretary says, you are anxious that arrests should be made in a manner and at a time when they are likely to cause the least disturbance, did the police wait until the people were assembled on a Sunday morning? The police were there 100 strong from 7 in the morning, why did they not effect the arrest at an early hour? They waited until he passed into church and until Divine Service was over. Perhaps the House is not aware that on that day Father McFadden, with the near prospect of his own arrest, addressed the people from the steps of the altar with as powerful an address in the interest of peace and on the duties of self-denial, forbearance, and Christian church. Divine Service being over, Father McFadden walked out, wearing his soutane and biretta, and carrying his breviary in his hand. Outside the door the people were collected, and the authorities could not have chosen a psychological moment more likely to provoke a riot. Inspector Martin, whose tragic death no man can deplore more deeply than my colleagues and myself— he was known to be a man of excitable disposition and should never have been sent on such an errand—came to the priest and seized him by the arm at the same moment drawing his sword, saying, "Come along with me." With the force used the priest's garment was torn, and as the sword flashed an excitable girl in the crowd cried out that the Inspector had struck the priest with his sword. Father McFadden asked for the authority for his arrest, and the warrant was produced. From that moment—and the evidence of the police is unanimous on this—Father McFadden did as he was desired, and went in the direction of his house, went on so fast indeed that he stumbled by the way. Father McFadden, as well as the officer, was struck in the burst of irrepressible uncontrollable fury which seized the people when, as they thought, they witnessed an attack upon their best friend and protector, whom they loved and almost worshipped. They rushed forward with the tragic result we all deplore. Father McFadden called out in English and Irish to the people to preserve peace and return to their homes. We have it from Father McFadden himself that in the course of his 10 years' administration of the parish he had never before in many crises found the people escape from his control, and the only occasion on which they failed to respond to his appeal was when he was powerless, because the people saw him made the victim of outrage. This holy priest, this devoted man who has given his time and his substance to the service of these poor and wretched people, stands charged with murder. Now, I beg the House of Commons to try and consider these things apart from all political feeling—I appeal to every Member, no matter what his political opinion, what is the possibility of convicting such a man, who all his life has behaved in the interests of peace and for the welfare of his people, of such a crime? The release of this priest is necessary for the preparation of the defence of the other persons accused, he is the one moral bulwark between the desperate people of his parish and the teachings of despair. I most unfeignedly declare that I have nothing but the interests of public peace at heart when I say that justice is outraged by the indefinite postponement of proceedings. If the Attorney General, having the evidence before him, finds it is not sufficient to sustain the charge, let him fulfil the duty he owes at once to justice and to his Government and withdraw the charge, giving thereby the best security he can for the preservation of peace in Donegal. How long is the military occupation of the country to continue? Forty-six men have been arrested; you hold 23 of them in prison. Every reasonable man, every lawyer, must be aware that this is far in excess of any number that can be criminally concerned. Cordons were drawn around an area of 16 miles, and soldiers and police dragged the country into a net, searching every house, stable, and field for evidence. The ordinary course of procedure is subverted; instead of collecting evidence and making arrests as suspicion pointed, the police swept the country with a drag net, and having got their prisoners then searched for evidence. The whole thing is scandalous to the last degree. We had a drunken constable on the witness table giving his testimony in a matter of life and death, but the magistrates saw nothing wrong until his ribaldry became so intolerable, they were obliged to censure him. We had a prisoner identified in the dock by a constable, and when the accused changed places with another, the constable a few minutes afterwards declared an entirely different person to be the same man. We have had a policeman who knew the names of prisoners telling them to the witnesses. We have had throughout the whole proceedings the most flagrant examples of that tendency among official witnesses to have less regard for truth and justice than esprit de corps, and the desire to procure convictions. What is to be the sequel? When is this system of oppression and military terrorism to cease? It is bad enough that these poor peasants should suffer hunger as the result of your system of rule; but if they must live in hunger, at least let them live in peace. Hunger and ease are the rights of a dog; but you not only condemn these poor people to starve, you deny them ease. The men have sought shelter in the mountains and caves, and so you institute a system of passes. I have heard of two men gathering seaweed being asked for passes—for their authority to be at work. They had no passes; they were taken to the police station and examined, and subsequently set at liberty; but they were fined for working without permission, for when they came back the tide had washed away the result of their day's labour—the seaweed they had collected. We have heard of midnight visits to the house of a poor woman who was in that condition that ought to excite the sympathy of any man. Three nights before the birth of her infant was, she visited, and again three nights afterwards. Upon her bed, which lay upon the ground, did the police trample in carelessness, in wantonness, or reckless search for something. The police went to the bed where the children were and turned down the clothes — we have all this on undoubted evidence—it is not sufficient to say it is not true—and finally they went to the bed of a girl of thirteen and held a gun to her head while they put a series of questions to her. Is this conciliation? Is this civilization? Is this the Unionist policy for Ireland; or is it rank, undiluted, revolting barbarism? I trust, at any rate, the arrests are completed; that, under these conditions of hunger and destitution, the people are at liberty to live, and that we have heard the last of these military cordons, domiciliary visits, and passes. It is high time that a district so scourged by nature should have relief from the terrorism of man. I wish Members would pay a visit to the district and see these miserable houses, built of mud and wattles, which are being levelled to the ground by the battering ram of self-defence. There is not on the face of the earth a district more bleak and stern. It has been well described by the correspondent of the Daily News. Whoever sees the place must be convinced a policy is being there pursued unworthy of a statesman, of a Christian, of a man—a policy repugnant to the feelings of humanity and the sense of justice dominant in the breasts of Englishmen; and I believe the British people will yet avenge on the Chief Secretary at the first opportunity the contempt with which he treats those principles they hold sacred, and which they endeavour to carry into effect all over the globe wherever the British Empire holds sway." (11)

The Irish Attorney General Peter O'Brien QC also known as 'Peter the Packer' because of his tendency to deliver jury's favourable to the prosecution, proceeded to ensure a jury of 12 men that had no connection to the Land League were chosen to prosecute Father McFadden. Eleven of these were Protestant, who O'Brien believed would be more amenable to convicting a priest.

The trial was now news all over the world and yet again McFadden had found friends in the unlikeliest of places. James Stuart MP read out a letter in parliament from a Donegal landlord supporting McFadden.

He wanted to show the injustice McFadden and the people of Gweedore were fighting against. He read the following into the House of Commons record:

"I hold in my hand a letter addressed to Father McFadden by a landlord in the neighbourhood of the Olphert estate. It is useless, to deal kindly any longer with these tenants. I am going to clear out the two townlands, and it is my land I want now. Remember, they are merely living on my land as long as I let them, and I will not regard cost in carrying out my plans. In doing this I am only following out the Scriptural precept that 'a man may do what he likes with his own.' I am determined on this, and in five or at the most ten years' time there will probably not be a single family left there."(12)

Stuart warned the house: "Father McFadden has been a rock of defence, and it is an example of the unjust system which the Donegal peasantry have been taught by our administration to identify with the Government of the Queen."(13)

On the 15th of October 1889, 150 men and women from Gweedore walked the 51 kilometres to Letterkenny train station and began the train journey to Dublin where, two days later, McFadden's trial began on the 17th of October. The British authorities were shocked by the worldwide positive reaction to Father McFadden and wanted a quick resolution and the matter put to rest.

With the first defendant, Jack Gallagher, in the dock, defence Barrister Tim Healey MP argued that the Gweedore community believed it was a grievous crime to attack a priest in his vestments and were only defending McFadden from attack.

The jury were also shown photographs from James Glass showing the grinding poverty and distress suffered by the people of Gweedore.

After two weeks the jury failed to agree on the guilt of Jack Gallagher and with the prospect of a long trial ahead, a compromise was sought to ensure the trial did not collapse.

The defence team met with the Attorney General and a plea bargain was agreed for all of the men and women on trial.

There were four conditions mandated by the prosecution:

First, all prisoners would plead guilty.

Second, no prisoner would be sentenced to death. Thirdly, Father McFadden would be released immediately.

Finally, 30 years prison sentence would be divided amongst convicted prisoners. The convicted served between six months to 10 years with hard labour in Mountjoy jail.

All the accused agreed to these conditions, except Canon McFadden, who wanted to share the fate of his parishioners. He was reluctantly convinced that this was the best deal available, and he was set free on a bond of £50.

In the aftermath of the sentencing, The Irish Times said the result was "an imperfect conclusion, when no one has been made amenable capitally for one of the most horrible and unprovoked murders that ever has been committed. . ." The paper said the trial had "been, in many places, a practice of most unjust attack upon the character of the police."(14)

Those who were still imprisoned in 1892, were released by the new Liberal government.

## THE EXILED PRIEST

McFadden returned to Gweedore but was soon sent to America to help raise funds for the new cathedral in Letterkenny. When he arrived in the United States in the spring of 1897, he received a rapturous welcome from his fellow Irish men and women who hailed him a hero of the land war campaign.

He spent a total of nearly three years in America over two periods visiting towns and cities all over the US. His fund-raising activities where so successful the building of the Cathedral was now assured. It is a sobering thought that the magnificent St Eunan's Cathedral in Letterkenny might not have been built as quickly if it was not for Canon McFadden and the tragic death of RIC Inspector Martin.

On McFadden's return from America, he was promoted to the parish priest of Inniskeel in Glenties Donegal.

In 1901 he left the Parish of Gweedore for his new home.

He spent 17 years working tirelessly for his parishioners but without any further conflict or controversy with the authorities.

Education remained his great passion and in his new parish he was responsible for the construction of three new national schools and the renovation and upgrading of many more.

He may have avoided controversy, but his iron rule of his parishioners continued and his strong hold over his parishioners was the catalyst for the Glenties novelist Patrick McGill's 1914 novel, Children of the Dead End, which has a damning portrait of a parish priest, Fr Devaney, who is based on Canon McFadden.

The novel condemned the exploitation of the poor by landlords and their agents, by gombeen men and by the police. But it also attacked the Catholic clergy for their ruthless control over their flock and for charges that they exacted from them, such as "funeral offerings".

In early 1917 he attended a home rule conference in

Belfast and shortly after his return he fell ill. He died aged 74 on the 18th of April 1917.

Canon McFadden was a complex man with strong views and short on patience with those whom he disagreed with. However, to this day he is viewed as a man who fought for the poor against injustice and who spoke up for the voiceless.

He is remembered by many as a hero who stood against the landlords and the British establishment and deserves the name the 'fighting priest of Gweedore'.

## Sources:

1. *Canon James McFadden: The patriot priest of Gweedore, Martin McFadden*
2. *Irish Times, August 1880*
3. *The Dictionary of Ulster Biography (newulsterbiography.co.uk)*
4. *Canon James McFadden: The patriot priest of Gweedore, Martin McFadden*
5. *5HC Deb, July 27, 1885, vol 300 cc47-8*
6. *www.irishcentral.com/roots/history/canon-james-mcfadden-fighting-priest-gweedore*
7. *Irish Times, August 2019*
8. *Irish Times, February 16, 1888*
9. *Canon James McFadden: The patriot priest of Gweedore, Martin McFadden*

10. *HC Deb, April 4, 1889, vol 334, c1589https://api.parliament.uk/historic-hansard/commons/1889/apr/04/ father-mfadden-column_1589*

11. *HC Deb, April 12, 1889, vol 335, cc374-422*

12. *HC Deb, April 12, 1889, vol 335, cc374-422*

13. *HC Deb, April 12, 1889, vol 335, cc374-422*

14. *Irish Times, November 1888*

# CHAPTER 3
# THE DONEGAL TAJ MAHAL—
# THE OLD CHURCH OF
# DUNLEWEY

The Taj Mahal is one of the seven wonders of the world and over eight million people a year visit this symbol of love, devotion and loss.

The Taj Mahal which means the "Crown of the Palace" is an ivory-white marble mausoleum on the south bank of the Yamuna river in the Indian city of Agra. Commissioned in 1632 by the Mughal emperor, Shah Jahan (reigned from 1628 to 1658). It was a memorial to house the tomb of his favourite wife, Mumtaz Mahal. It was completed in 1653.

Two hundred years later, another monument to love and loss would be completed by a grieving spouse this time in Ireland and in County Donegal, that of the old church of Dunlewey.

It lies silently at the foot of Mount Errigal, the tallest of the Derryveagh mountain range and the largest in

Donegal. A beautiful building, it is a lasting memorial to a great love affair. That of James Russell once the landlord of the Dunlewey estate in Donegal and his wife Jane.

James Russell married Jane Smith in 1825 and they set up married life in London. James would go on to make a fortune as a hops merchant supplying the expanding brewing industry. They would be blessed with five daughters – Fannie, Henrietta, Emma, Louisa Sarah, and Josephine.

Using the wealth, they had acquired in London, the couple decided to leave England and purchase the Dunlewey estate, an area of sheep, lakes and outstanding natural beauty with the wild Atlantic to the west and the Derryveagh mountains to the east.

The estate was recorded as consisting of a house, outbuildings, gate lodges and 3825 acres of land, a large holding by the standards of the day.

Little is written of their time in Dunlewey, but James died on the 2nd of September 1848.

Heartbroken, his widow decided to build a church as a lasting monument for her husband.

Like the Taj Mahal, the Church of Ireland building was constructed at the foot of Errigal mountain using white marble but also blue quartzite which was quarried locally. The supply of marble in the nearby quarry has now been depleted. The red brick in the arches of the windows were produced locally. Remnants of the brick-field are still visible near Oilean Ghrainne when the level of the Dunlewey Lake has lowered.

James Russell was laid to rest in a vault under the church floor.

On the 1st of September 1853 the Church was consecrated as a chapel of Ease to the Church of Ireland in Tullaghbegley which was the parish consisting of the modern-day parishes of Gweedore and Cloughaneely.

The church is nestled in the valley between Errigal and the Poison Glen an area of stunning beauty and with a long history.

Whilst ominous sounding now, the Poison Glen may have been given the wrong name!

One story is that the wrong translation from Irish to English caused the confusion, and the correct name should be 'Heavenly Glen' (the Irish word for Heaven is neamh and the Irish word for poison is neimhe).

One other reason could be that the Poisoned Glen owes its name to the former presence of the highly toxic Irish Spurge Moss.

It is rumoured that the plant poisoned the drinking water and although the Spurge Moss is now extinct here farmers are still advised to keep their animals away from the Glen's waters.

I prefer to think folklore has given the glen its striking name. The story from lore is that the one-eyed king of Tory, Balor of the evil eye, had a beautiful daughter, Ethniu, who he kept locked away in a tower, out of men's view.

This was because he had been forewarned that only his grandson could end his life.

However, word of her beauty spread, and she was kidnapped and brought to the nearby mainland at Magheroarty.

Balor in a fury followed and caught up with her kidnappers at the entrance to the glen. He rescued his daughter and killed her kidnapper with a giant stone.

To this day one such stone stands in the glen and is said by locals to be the poisoned eye of Balor who has given his name to the glen where the old church of Dunlewey now lies.

With emigration and the decline in the Dunlewey estate, the population plummeted as did the congregation of the Dunlewey church. Gradually neglect and the elements took their eventual toll.

In 1955 the roof had deteriorated to such an extent that it was decided to remove it as a safety measure. The fixtures and fitting of the church were distributed to other churches throughout the Church of Ireland diocese of Derry and Raphoe. The bell was also removed and is now installed in the Cashel Church of Ireland near Doe Castle.

In 1987 the local community restored the floor. In

2005, half a century after the roof was removed work began so that this beautiful and historic landmark was preserved for future generations.

The church now stands roofless but sturdy, a popular tourist attraction and a poignant reminder of an enduring love.

The poignancy does not end with the grief of Jane Russell, another landlord of the estate Richard Lewis Crankshaw who died on the 29th of November 1929 is buried in the grounds of the old church of Dunlewey but without his wife.

His widow Nellie was a Roman Catholic and when she died in 1946, she was buried in the graveyard of the Sacred Heart Roman Catholic church which lies just across the lake in sight of the old church.

If you visit the Sacred Heart church you will see one gravestone turned towards the old church of Dunlewey, that's Mary Crankshaw who wished to be buried in sight of her husband facing his grave. The other headstones point away from the old church.

So, when you are in the Gweedore area make sure to visit the Donegal Taj Mahal a monument to love and loss, the 'old church of Dunlewey'.

# CHAPTER 4
# CROMWELLIAN MASSACRE
# OF RAY

The largest medieval stone cross in Ireland lies in the townland of Ray just outside the town of Falcarragh in county Donegal along the Wild Atlantic Way.

Saint Colmcille's cross stands 5.56m (18.2FT) high and 2.26m (7ft 5in) across. It is made of Muckish slate.

Standing in the ruins of the Church of Ray, the cross has an ancient history and has witnessed saints and the slaughter of an entire congregation by Cromwellian soldiers.

Historians believe that the first church of Ray was founded by St Fionán in the sixth century, this may have merit given his tendency for travel and reported zeal for establishing churches.

Folklore tells a tale that the cross was sculpted from a solid rock quarried on Muckish mountain and was originally commissioned by St Colmcille (521-597) to be erected on Tory Island.

Colmcille was born at Gartan, near Letterkenny in 521. He was also known as Columba, a Latin version of Colum, which was his baptismal name. The 'Cille' that was added to the end of his name means 'of the churches'.

His father was a great grandson of King Niall of the Nine Hostages. His mother was a daughter of the King of Leinster. Colmcille was first educated in Kilmacrennan by Cruitnechan, who had baptised him. Colmcille went to St Finnian's monastic school in Movilla, Co. Down. He later continued his education at Clonard monastery in Co. Meath.(1)

In 545, Colmcille founded his first monastery in Derry. He went on to create over sixty monasteries and churches in Ireland and Scotland.

He also established a monastery on Tory Island just off the coast of northwest Donegal and the legend goes that the stone cross that now resides in Ray was destined for the island.

However, St Colmcille instead gave it as a gift to the Fionán, who legend says miraculously retrieved Colmcille's treasured prayer book.

Colmcille had travelled from the mainland to Tory Island with his two companions Saints Fionán and Begley. Once they arrived on the island, Colmcille realised that he had left his prayer book on the mainland. He asked his companions if one of them would return to find the prayer book. Whoever returned would be given anything he desired. St Fionán went back to the mainland and found an eagle sheltering the prayer book from the rain with his outstretched wings. Fionán took the prayer book back to Tory and asked for the cross in return. Colmcille is said to have been displeased but kept his promise by granting Fionán his wish and the cross ended up not in Tory but on the mainland.(2)

There has always been confusion regarding which Fionán was involved, it was most likely the cross was gifted to Fionán of Clonard rather than St Finnian of Movilla, who would eventually become the catalyst for St Colmcille journey to Iona.

In 560 St Colmcille became embroiled in an argument with St Finnian of Movilla regarding a Psalter which is a book of psalms.

St Colmcille copied the manuscript at the scriptorium under Finnian, intending to keep the copy. Finnian disputed his right to keep it.

The High King Diarmuid was asked to determine the owner of the copy. He famously ruled as follows: 'To every cow her calf and to every book its copy.' This gave ownership to Saint Finnian.(3)

There is a suggestion that this conflict resulted in the

Battle of Cúl Dreimhne in Cairbre Drom Cliabh (now in County Sligo) around 561.

Over 3,000 warriors were killed in the battle. As a penance, Colmcille left Ireland forever eventually founding the monastery on Iona in 563 which became the cradle of the Celtic church in the kingdom of Dalriada which would eventually become Scotland.

Alas this tale regarding the Crosses origins is but legend, as the cross has been dated to the 8th century, well after the time of Saints Colmcille and Fionán.(4)

Despite this, there is a clear link with Iona, the final resting place of Colmcille, as the cross is virtually identical to the Saint John's Cross on Iona which dates from the same period.

The cross in Ray stood until it was knocked down in a storm in 1750.

Given the anti-Irish and Catholic bias and punitive penal laws it was no surprise the cross was neglected. It would remain almost forgotten and broken in two pieces for 220 years.

This was until the Donegal office of public works decided to restore the cross in 1970.

The cross is now held together by two metal strips and back in one piece, it stands majestic in the ruined church of Ray. The church itself stands on the east bank of the river Ray and near its estuary.

From the 6th to the 8th centuries the river was a

boundary between two small kingdoms, the Cineál Duach on the east of the river and the Cineál Lughdach on the west. The connections between Iona and Ray are further strengthened by the fact that in the 7th century no fewer than four important abbots of Iona came from the Cineál Duach. Almost certainly, this was their home church.

The great high cross now stands inside the ruins which date mainly from the 17th century.

The Roman Catholic church of Ray survived in various guises until the coming of Oliver Cromwell and the parliamentary army.

The English parliamentary forces were concerned about the Irish Catholic Confederation, which controlled most of Ireland, and who had just made an alliance with the English Royalists and declared Charles II King of Ireland. This Confederate policy did imply at least the strong possibility, sooner or later, of an Irish-based Royalist invasion of England.

Historians offer other reasons for the invasion of the Cromwellian forces such as: The Parliament was dominated by hard-line protestant fundamentalists, who saw the "papist" Irish Confederation as a religious threat. In that regard, something of a continuation of the wars of religion on the continent.

Also a desire to support the protestant Scots and English settlers/colonists in the Plantation areas, who had been on the receiving end of quite a lot of violence during the previous 10 years.

One more pressing need may have been the fact that the civil war had driven England to the point of bankruptcy and an invasion of Ireland was profitable. There was in many a desire for more Irish land that could be seized to sell / gift, to help finance Parliament's debts.

On 13th August 1649 Oliver Cromwell and a flotilla of around 35 ships sailed from Milford Haven to Dublin. Cromwell spent most of the voyage being seasick. A second, larger fleet of approximately 84 vessels sailed the next day and arrived at Dublin after adverse weather prevented them from landing in Munster. A third, smaller flotilla came into Dublin a few days later. With his forces safely landed at Dublin, Cromwell marched his army into the field. In September and October 1649, he stormed the towns of Drogheda and Wexford. In his justification for the massacre that took place at Wexford Cromwell blamed the privateering actions of the inhabitants, writing that:

'. . . yet God would not have it so, but by an unexpected providence, in his righteous justice, brought a just judgement upon them, causing them to become a prey to the soldier, who in their pyracies had made preys of so many families, and made with their bloods to answer the cruelties which they had exercised upon the lives of divers poor Protestants'.(5)

Despite Cromwell's victories in the autumn of 1649, the war dragged on and in 1650, the Cromwellian forces routed the catholic Ulster army at the battle of Scarrifholis.

On the 21st of June 1650, the Irish Confederate army commanded by Herbert MacMahon the Roman Catholic Bishop of Clogher, faced the Cromwellian New Model Army and local ulster protestant settlers led by Charles Coote, 1st Earl of Mountrath.

The Catholic army was annihilated and lost most of its weapons and supplies. This catastrophic defeat secured the North of Ireland for the New Model Army and was a major factor in the Cromwellian conquest of Ireland.

The war would soon impact the Church of Ray which was destroyed by a platoon of Cromwellian soldiers under the command of Captain Robert Cunnyngham in late 1651.

Cunnyngham was the Constable of Doe Castle, which had been captured in 1650 by Cromwellian forces from Derry.

Robert Cunnyngham led a platoon of soldiers to commit an atrocity against the Catholic worshipers of Ray church, whom they believed to be heretics.

The Cromwellian soldiers approached the church and while the congregation was gathered inside hearing mass, they burst open the doors.

The entire congregation was slaughtered including the priest, in what was to become known as the 'Massacre of Ray' (Marfach Raithe).

The bodies of the dead were buried in a mass grave within two hundred meters of the church at a place called 'Resting place of the Bones' (Lag Na gCnamh).

The church no longer Roman Catholic continued to be used by the Church of Ireland until the early 19Th century, until it fell into its present state of decay and disrepair. Several gravestones scatter the grounds, many from the Olphert family, local landlords of the time. The Olphert 18,133-Acre estate surrounded Falcarragh and Ardsmore, north of Gweedore. The Olpherts where descended from a Dutch Protestant who had bought the property in 1661.(6)

The Church of Ray now stands as a ruin, just off the N56 on the Falcarragh to Ballyboe road and is well worth a visit. I'd urge you all to seek it out when in the local area. As for Robert Cunnyngham, he continued his murderous campaign of religious genocide and was involved in the massacre of 83 catholic men, women and children on the Island of Arranmore.

He met his end at the hands of two vengeful survivors from the Arranmore massacre when he was stabbed to death at Cashelmore, near Ards (Creeslough) in revenge for his bloody exploits on the island.

**Sources:**

1. *Sli - St Columba Trail (colmcille.org)*
2. *www.falcarraghvisitorcentre.com/ray-cross-folklore- archaeology-and-historical-context*
3. *www.libraryireland.com/biography/ SaintColumcille*
4. *www.falcarraghvisitorcentre.com/ray-cross-folklore- archaeology-and-historical-context*
5. *History Ireland, Issue 4 (July/August 2011), Volume 19*
6. *The landlord in Donegal: Pictures from the Wilds, Denis Holland, 1858*

# CHAPTER 5
# THE SINKING OF THE HMS WASP

I n September 1884, a royal navy gunboat on route to carry out an eviction sunk off the coast of Tory Island in Donegal. Smashed on to rocks, she sank in just 15 minutes and 52 men perished. The official cause of the sinking was due to negligence, but rumour and folklore persist that sabotage or even a curse could be responsible for the sinking of HMS Wasp.

Ireland in 1884 was a nation in turmoil, the scars of the great famine were still raw, two years previously the two most senior politicians in Ireland had been assassinated by the Invincible's in the Phoenix park and the land war still raged all across the island.

The land war was organised by the Land League, spearheaded by the great Irish patriot Michael Davitt. The Land League had three simple but profoundly important demands which became known as the 3 Fs: fair rent, free sale, and fixity of tenure.

The landlords were mostly Angelo Irish and many of those where absentees, living in England or Scotland in great style, while their tenants suffered in poverty trying to scratch out a living in areas suffering from great neglect, as the absentee landlords refused to invest in their properties that many of them would seldom see or visit.

It was no wonder that Ireland was suffering a period of extreme social upheaval and unrest.

It was in this atmosphere that HMS Wasp began her final journey from her home port of Westport in County Mayo to facilitate the eviction of three tenant families on the Island of Inishtrahull, which is the most northerly of the Irish islands, lying six miles from Malin Head off the coast of county Donegal. Though uninhabited now, the last residents having left in 1929, the island supported several tenant families in the 1880s as well as a lighthouse.

Commissioned on 1st December 1881, HMS Wasp was a Banterer class gunboat built for colonial service throughout the British Empire, to enforce what became known as 'gunboat diplomacy'.

She was 125 feet long and displaced 465 tons. A 360 Horsepower steam engine gave a top speed of a mere 9.5

knots. This made the Wasp a workhorse rather than a racehorse and the engine was supplemented by a rigging system carried on three masts to aid the engine or to replace it when the ship had to conserve coal on long voyages.

For their size, these vessels carried a heavy armament – they had two 6-inch 64-pounder muzzle-loading rifles, supplemented by two 4-inch breech-loaders as well as small-calibre maxims, gardners or gatlings. The unsophisticated 6-inch weapons were effective enough for shore bombardment and the vessel's small size and sailing ability made them useful for colonial duties, for which armour was not required.(1)

The Wasp began her active service, stationed in what was then called Queenstown, which we now know as Cobh county Cork. Little is known of the Wasps earlier duties, but they are likely to have been fishery inspection and lighthouse provision throughout the Irish coastal waters.

The crew compliment of the Wasp was 60 officers and men. In 1884, as the agitation of the Land war grew, she was moved to Westport to help quell civil disobedience and as a symbol of imperial power in a region which was a hotbed of civil unrest.

The Wasp commanded by 39-year-old Lieutenant JD Nicholls was ordered to report to Moville in County

Donegal to pick up Bailiffs and Police, whom an absentee landlord had ordered to evict three tenant families, who had refused to or more likely where unable to pay their rent on Inishtrahull.

Evictions at the time saw large deployments of armed police and in some cases the military to protect the bailiffs who carried out these inhuman evictions.

A particularly nasty element of the evictions process was the destruction of the families' house by battering ram so that they could not return. There are many poignant photographs that show the horror and the brutality of these land war era evictions.

## A FINAL FATEFUL JOURNEY

So, on September 21st, 1884, HMS Wasp left Westport to facilitate yet another eviction of poor farming families from their homes. Ironically, this was not the Wasps first visit to Inishtrahull, the year previously they had delivered a cargo of seed potatoes to the islanders donated by the Quakers Society of Friends.

In 1883 the Wasp had also delivered the soldiers to Sheephaven who were stationed near Dunfanaghy during the Land League agitation campaign in Donegal.

HMS Wasp did not appear to be in a hurry, as she was under sail and her steam engine was turned off.

In the early hours of the 22nd of September, she was

sailing nine miles off the coast of Northwest Donegal and the island of Tory.

The weather was not classed as stormy or indeed hazardous. It was reported at Mullaghmore in Donegal bay, the nearest meteorological station to Tory Island, that the weather on Sunday night before the disaster was clear with a fresh westerly breeze and sky overcast.(2)

It would later be reported that one of the crew remarked to Lieutenant Nicholls before he retired, that the vessel was heading for the Tory lighthouse and this course should be altered. This could not be changed quickly as the vessel was not under steam but sail. The commanding officer replied that the ship was keeping the course he had marked out on the chart which would prove quite safe.(3)

Nicholls like most of the crew including his other officers were now sleeping in their bunks.

Naval historians have always questioned why the Wasp was sailing inside Tory rather than out to her west, which would have given the ship greater sea room. Also being under sail meant she did not have the manoeuvrability that her steam engine would have provided.

The Wasp was well known in the waters but the navigator on duty was comparatively inexperienced as to the dangers of the Donegal coast and was unfamiliar with the terrain around Tory.

One of the officers ordered a sail to be shortened just

before the gun boat struck the rocks, a sea man who survived told the officer this action would surely land her upon the rocks but he was ordered to shorten the sail and he obeyed.(4)

At 3.55am the ship struck a reef directly under the Tory lighthouse.

The light house stands on the north side of the island. It was erected in 1832. The tower is 27m high and the light is 40m above sea level and may be seen for eighteen nautical miles when the atmosphere is clear. Reefs of rocks, portions of which are not visible at high water abound on the west coast in front of the island.(5)

The initial collusion broke the hull of the Wasp in two and she began to take on water at an alarming rate. Awoken from his slumber, the ships commander Lieutenant Nicholls ordered the crew to take to the lifeboats. However, disaster struck, and the Wasp hit the reefs again. There was no hope for HMS Wasp as the impact shattered what was left of the ship and within 15 minutes the Wasp was under water with only her masthead protruding from the Atlantic waves.

Five survivors clung to a spur of the gun boat which had detached from the wreck and were washed up on the rocks. One lucky man had a miraculous event when the ill-fated ship cantered over, and he jumped from the rigging directly onto the rocks below.

The Quartermaster of the Wasp was saved, as was the man on look out on the forecastle (the forward part of a ship below the deck, traditionally used as the crew's living quarters).  Also among the three other survivors were the man at the wheel and two marines. No islanders saw the wreck happen and the light keeper was only alerted later by the cries of the drowning.

Fifty-two of the HMS Wasp crew including Lieutenant Nicholls sadly perished.

The Belfast Morning News who sent a correspondent to cover the tragedy printed a perspective of the disaster from a Tory islander interviewed in Gweedore just three days after the sinking:

"I was in conversation today with a Tory islander who had met one of the six survivors of the Wasp disaster. All are in fair condition having only sustained slight wounds on the rocks. The ill-fated ship almost cantered over on to the rocky shore as one of the survivors jumped from her rigging onto the rocks without entering the water at all. The others saved can hardly tell how they got onto land. It was due more to waves washing them up than anything else. No bodies have yet washed ashore or been recovered. The cries were heard at the light house which was within about 200 yards of the spot. The light keeper and his assistant came towards the cries, and they were met by two of the men who escaped outside of the light house wall".(6)

The survivors stayed on Tory for four days well cared for by the islanders until a navy frigate HMS Valiant took them to Rathmullan.

Admiral Sethbridge at Queenstown received the following telegraph from the chief officer at Sheephaven Dunfanaghy:

"Lord Leitrim sent his steamer Norsemen to Tory Island. Men saved from Wasp refused to leave Tory until officially ordered. Men suffering from wounds received in landings. Master of Norsemen landed his mate at noon. Valiant passed going towards Tory island at 2.30 this afternoon".(7)

After arriving in Rathmullan the survivors were moved on to Derry where they were treated as celebrities by a large crowd, even meeting the Mayor at the time Mr McVicker. After a short stay in Dublin the six survivors were summoned to Portsmouth for a court martial.

A royal navy court of enquiry found that HMS Wasp had been lost: "In consequence of the want of due care and attention" All of the survivors were exonerated.

No one, not even the sleeping Nicholls and his officers were given the blame for the sinking and the court martial verdict was consigned to history.

However, historians and others have speculated that the cause of the sinking could be related to either the Tory Lighthouse or even a curse!

## WAS THE LIGHT HOUSE LIGHT TURNED OFF?

The lighthouse theory speculates that there must have been someone or a group of people bearing ill intent towards the crew of the HMS Wasp.

Tory had a large Fenian contingent among the population, including the elected king of the island a man called Heggarty, who along with many on the island had feared that the Wasp was on route to Tory for evictions rather than Inishtrahull. Perhaps Heggarty and the islanders were intent on resisting any evictions that might be planned.

What we do know from survivor reports is that the lighthouse was on after the collision, but could it have been switched off before the Wasp struck the reef?

Some speculate that given the navigational skills of Lieutenant Nicholls it is unlikely that the ship would crash if there was a proper light source such as from Tory.

Lieutenant Nicholls was a well-respected sea man

with a track record of successfully navigating the dangerous waters of the northwest, and this was reinforced by a resolution passed by the piers and Harbour's commissioners' days after the disaster:

> "Today at a meeting of the piers and harbours commissioners held at the castle, Col Nolan MP in the chair, a resolution was passed expressing the regret of the commissioners at the death of Commander Nicholls and of his officers and crew of the Wasp and bearing testimony to the care skill and efficiency with which the vessel was navigated by Commander Nicholls during the recent inspection of commissioners on the west coast of Ireland".(8)

The fact that the lighthouse light was never mentioned at the court martial does suggest to me that it did not play a major role in the sinking of the Wasp. Also, while the Light House theory has its adherents, I would have to discount it due to no hard evidence of any collusion.

## WAS IT A CURSE?

One other theory or perhaps local folklore is that HMS Wasp was sunk through the use of the Tory Island cursing stone, once again by islander's fearful of a future eviction themselves. Tory did indeed have such a stone at the time called 'Cloch na Mallacht' or 'Cloch Thorai'. Folklore links the stone to St Colmcille and the pilgrimage route around the island 'An Turas Mor'.

Pilgrims would visit the numerous holy sites on Tory and then at the end of their walk they would defiantly turn the cursing stone upside down. However, a curse could be invoked if the pilgrimage route was done in a counter clockwise direction. Folklore notes that such a curse helped defeat an earlier invading English raiding party.

No matter if you believe in curses or not, one fact we do know is that the cursing stone disappeared shortly after the sinking of the Wasp. The local priest Fr Michael O'Donnell had it removed, and to this present day, no one knows or perhaps is willing to tell where it is.(9)

The Admiralty court martial did not blame any one person in particular for the loss of the Wasp but instead pronounced the tragedy was: "In consequence of the want of due care and attention".

I tend to believe that three factors contributed to the sinking oi the Wasp.


1. **The unpredictable weather:** The waters of the North Atlantic off the coast of Tory are

notoriously dangerous and despite the forecast mild weather, hours before the Wasp sank, another tragedy took place when a local fishing boat capsized just miles from Tory. A boat containing three local fishermen capsized near the area wherethe Wasp went down and two of the men drowned, Morgan Sweeney and Hugh O'Donnell. The brother of Hugh O'Donnell managed to swim to shore.

2. **Inexperience and negligence:** While there is no disputing the evidence that Lieutenant Nicholl was an experienced navigator, who had great knowledge of the waters around Tory, he was in bed asleep when the boat sank. The officer of the watch was completely unaware of the dangers that lay ahead. Could a more experienced sea man have perhaps steered the ship to safety?

3. **Complacency:** The Wasp was under sail when she sank. She would have had more manoeuvrability and speed if she were utilising her steam engines. Was the fact she was under sail complacency or perhaps a cost cutting exercise?

These three factors, all with evidence to back them up, are far more powerful reasons for the sinking of HMS

Wasp than a Tory conspiracy or a curse. However, no matter the reason for the sinking, we must remember the 52 men who lost their lives in this tragedy.

Over the next few weeks after the sinking, bodies of the deceased came ashore across the Donegal coastline, and many are buried in many local graveyards from Gweedore to Malin Head. A monument was later erected on the mainland in the church yard of St Ann's Church of Ireland in Killut, near Gort an Choirce, where several crew members are buried.

This is a most poignant memorial, as it looks out to Tory and the site of the sinking of HMS Wasp, which never did help evict poor Irish farmers from their homes on Inishtrahull.

The islanders of Inishtrahull, were reprieved from eviction, and remained on the island until 1929.

I'd like to leave you with a tribute to the men of HMS Wasp from the Society of Friends in a letter to the Belfast Morning News on 24th September 1884.

"Sir, in reference to the sad calamity that has occurred to HMS Wasp off Tory Island, we are honorary secretaries to the fund promoted last year by the society of friends for supplying potatoes to the distressed peasantry of County Donegal desire to express our deep feelings of regret at the disaster.

For several weeks during the spring of 1883, we

and other members of the committee were more or less engaged in sailing around the dangerous coast of Donegal chiefly in the Wasp and in her twice visiting Tory Island. In memory of Lieutenant Commander Nicholls and those under him we wish to recall the kindness, courtesy and the zeal they displayed in the efforts made to relieve distress, the men willingly undergoing much hard work and dirty work in loading and unloading the vessel.

Great sympathy will be felt towards the relatives of those that are lost especially so by the committee and the subscribers of the fund we have mentioned, and we feel sure that in the cheerless cabins of Donegal will arise a profound feeling of regret at the sad fate of those who did much to help them in their time of need".

Yours truly

John Pim and John Marsh Society of Friends(10)

## Sources:

1. *Dawlish Chronicles*
2. *Belfast Morning News, September 25, 1884*
3. *Belfast Morning News, September 25, 1884*
4. *Belfast Morning News, September 25, 1884*
5. *irishlights.ie*
6. *Belfast Morning News, September 25, 1884*

7. *Press Association, September 1884*

8. *Belfast Morning News, September 25, 1884*

9. *Tory Island and the Cursing Stones, DailyScribblings.com*

10. *Belfast Morning News, September 25, 1884*

# CHAPTER 6
# BALOR—THE PIRATE OF TORY ISLAND

The drive towards Mount Errigal along the R251 is one of the most spectacular in Ireland. Not only do you pass through the picturesque village of Dunlewey (Dún Lúiche) with its shimmering lake and old church, but you also gaze upon one of Ireland's natural wonders full of history and beauty, the Poisoned Glen.

The Poisoned Glen lies at the foot of Mount Errigal, the tallest peak of the Derryveagh mountain range, in Dunlewey part of Gweedore in the Donegal Gaeltacht.

The Derryveagh mountain range, or as it is referred to by the locals the 'Seven Sisters', includes the mountains of; Aghla Beg, Aghla More, Ardloughnabrackbaddy, Crocknalaragagh, Errigal, Mackoght (known also as little Errigal) and Muckish.

The Poisoned Glen is also a much-visited venue for

mountaineering and rock climbing as it has the Bearnas Buttress, which is Ireland's largest continual rock face.

Many people have wondered why an area of such breath-taking beauty would be called the Poisoned Glen. A story gaining more and more traction is that it was wrongly translated from Irish to English long ago and in reality, it should be called the 'Heavenly Glen". This is because the Irish word for Heaven is 'neamh' and the Irish word for poison is 'neimhe'. So, you can see how a mistake could be made.

However, the story I prefer regarding its name involves the notorious pirate and war lord of folklore Balor of the evil eye.

Balor was the grandson of Neit who was a god of war. He was the warlord and king of the Formorians, the grotesque race that inhabited Ireland before the coming of Tuatha de Dannan, The tribe of Danu. In Irish mythology, Balor can be equated to a god of death and destruction.

He became known as 'Balor of the Evil Eye' after he was caught spying on druids preparing a draught of wisdom; some of the potion splashed on to one of his eyes, which made his stare devastatingly harmful to all those he looked upon. He kept his evil eye closed when not in battle, and his lid was so heavy that he needed four attendants to lift it.

Balor, lived on the Island of Tory off the west coast of

what is now County Donegal, and had a very beautiful daughter Ethniu who he kept hidden away in a tower out of men's view.

However, word of her beauty spread, and she was kidnapped and brought to Magheroarty on the mainland. In a rage Balor followed determined to retrieve his daughter. He pursued her captors catching up with them at the entrance to what is now the Poisoned Glen. He picked up a giant stone and crushed her kidnappers. This stone still stands, and it is said to be the poisoned eye of Balor.

The story of Balor goes beyond Donegal, Tory and the Poisoned Glen. Essentially it is a tale of good versus evil, of light banishing darkness and a rebirth of Ireland from chaos and disruption.

Called the king of demons.by his enemies Balor was a giant with an eye in the middle of his forehead. He was undefeated in battle as no army could withstand the force of his eye when it was opened. His four retainers who accompanied him at all times had only one job which was to raise his eyelid in the heat of battle.

Because of its destructive force Balor is often depicted wearing an eye patch. Other folklore sources describe his eye as follows:

"It was always covered with seven cloaks to keep it cool. He took the cloaks off one by one. At the first, ferns began to wither. At the second, grass began to redden. At the third, wood and trees began to heat up. At the fourth, smoke came out of wood and trees. At the fifth, everything got red hot. At the sixth the land would quake. At the seventh, the whole land caught fire".

Balor was a very superstitious being. He lived his live by one great prophecy that he could only be killed by his own Grandson. This is why he kept his only child Ethniu imprisoned in the high tower on his strong hold of Tory Island.

As Ethniu grew into a beautiful young woman unsure why she remained imprisoned Balor caused havoc plundering boats and constantly raiding the mainland.

While we have seen in the story of the Poisoned Glen that Ethniu was freed once and recaptured, she remained imprisoned and there she stayed until Balor made a fateful mistake.

Being the pirate, he was Balor, led a raid on the mainland to steal the 'Glas Gaibhnenn' the white cow of plenty. A mystical animal that supplied unending and copious amounts of milk.

This Cow was owned by the chief of nearby Tullaghobegly MacKineely.

Using magic to transform himself into a red-haired

boy, he tricked the warrior Cian who was a brother of MacKineely into giving him the cow.

Balors raid stole the cow, and he took it back to Tory. The place where the cow was dragged ashore is still called Port Na Glaise or Cow Harbour.

The warrior Cian who was tasked with guarding the cow was distraught at the loss of the Cow to the tribe and deeply ashamed he resolved to get the animal back from Balor.

On his quest he sought the help of the Druidess Birog. She told Cian that the Cow could never be retrieved while Balor lived, so it was time for an alternative plan, and he resolved to give Balor grandchildren. This would help fulfil the prophesy that Balor could only die at the hands of his grandson. With his death the Cow could eventually be returned.

With the help of Birog and fair winds granted by the sea god Manannan, Cian was blown onto Tory and climbed the high tower imprisoning Balor's daughter Ethniu.

They made love and Ethniu subsequently gave birth to three sons.

When Balor discovered his daughter was pregnant, he flew into a rage and when Ethniu gave birth to three sons Balor was steadfast in his resolve that to prevent the prophesy his grandsons must die.

They were thrown into the wild seas, while two died,

one was rescued by the sea god Manannan and raised as his son and given the name Lugh.

While Lugh grew to manhood protected by Manannan, the power of the Formorians and Balor grew.

Legend tells us that the Tuatha De Danann the rulers of Ireland fell under the heel of the undefeatable Balor and the expanding evil Formorians. They decided to take a stand and fight for their freedom.

Lebor Gabala Erenn 'the book of invasions of Ireland' informs us of the Tuatha De Danann losing the first battle and regrouping for vengeance.

Lugh who is both Formorian through his mother and of the Tuatha De Danann through his father Cian was asked by the king Nuada to lead the Tuatha De Danann army as they prepared for a second battle.

The fight did not begin well for the Tuatha De Danann. Balor removed his seven cloaks, and his four attendants lifted the eyelid of his magical eye unleashing carnage on the battlefield.

In the fray the Tuatha De Danann king Nuada was killed by Balor.

Now the famed prophesy Balor did so much to avert began to unfold.

Lugh the grandson of Balor took aim with his sling and like David slew the evil goliath that was Balor.

A rock smashed into his eye thrusting it into the back

of his head and his frightening gaze reflected back upon the Formorian army reducing them to dust.

One other legend tells a tale that, when Balor was slain by Lugh, his eye was still open when he fell face first into the ground. Thus, his deadly eye beam burned a hole into the earth.

Long after, the hole filled with water and became a lake which is now known as Loch na Súil, or "Lake of the Eye", in County Sligo.

Lugh eventually became the king of the Tuatha De Danann whose victory over the Formorians meant they reigned over Ireland until their battles with the Fir Bolg, but that is another tale for another time.

# CHAPTER 7
# VINCENT 'MAD DOG' COLL— THE GANGSTER FROM GWEEDORE

One of the most notorious Irish gangsters of the prohibition era was Vincent 'Mad Dog' Coll. A handsome and intelligent man, he was also a cold-hearted killer who some believed was psychotic and in his short life he left a legacy of gang land killings, kidnapping and the murder of a five-year-old child. This is his story.

Vincent Coll was born on July 20th, 1908 in the Irish-speaking parish of Gweedore which, at the time, was an impoverished region of County Donegal. Gweedore was rich in beauty but lacking in opportunities and employment and its biggest industry in 1908 was emigration.

When Vincent was less than a year old, his parents decided to do what many Irish people did in those days, they emigrated to America to seek a better life. With their seven children, the Colls settled in the Irish enclave of the Bronx but found that their lives in New York were not much better than the one that they had left behind in Gweedore.

They still lived in dire poverty, leading Coll's father to eventually desert the family. Coll's mother and all but one of his six siblings died before he turned 12 years old. After his mother died, Coll and his brother Peter were placed in a number of Catholic orphanages but were found to be uncontrollable by the clergy who ran these institutions.

Eventually the Coll brothers were sent to live with an aunt named Mary Friel in Hell's Kitchen another native of Gweedore.

If the authorities thought that living with a close relative would turn the boys into law-abiding citizens, they were sorely mistaken. The brothers used the Friel home as a base from which they organised a juvenile street gang made up mainly of Italian youths who had dreams of becoming Mafiosi, like the leading Italian gangsters who were beginning to make a name for themselves in New York City.

Vincent was a difficult child, constantly in trouble and he was expelled from several local Catholic schools before he even reached his teens. On the streets he had swapped formal education for another form of learning — the art of crime, with a local gang called the Gophers, led by Owen 'Owney' Madden.(1)

## TURNING TO CRIME

While schoolbooks had been no attraction, Coll was a fast learner in the art of crime and he soon came to the attention of the established gangster, Arthur Flegenheimer, better known as 'Dutch Schultz.'

Shultz was a Jewish-American mob leader who had amassed power and wealth through 'bootlegging' (producing and selling illegal alcohol) and the 'numbers' or illegal gambling, racket.

While criminal gangs grew rich controlling gambling, prostitution and protection rackets, the catalyst for the growth of organised crime in the US was the exploitation of the prohibition of Alcohol. On October 28th, 1919, the US Congress passed the Volstead Act, the popular name for the National Prohibition Act.

This established the legal definition of intoxicating liquors as well as penalties for producing them. Although the Volstead Act prohibited the sale of alcohol, the federal government lacked resources to enforce It and criminal gangs began to meet the continuing demand for liqueur, amassing massive profits and influence in the process.

In the violent poverty-stricken era of 1920s New York, Coll was not afraid to do whatever it took to rise to the top of the gangster tree. His aggressive and volatile personality made him a man to be feared and his willingness to murder to get what he wanted made him a trusted lieutenant of Schultz. He soon became one of the Prohibition era's most feared enforcers. He had no qualms about using violence and was a ruthless killer.

As the body count rose, the authorities started to take a keen interest in Coll.

In 1927, at just 19, Vincent Coll was accused of the murder of a 'speakeasy' (illegal tavern) owner who had refused to sell bootleg alcohol for Dutch Schultz.

Coll was found not guilty and acquitted, which was no surprise as Schultz used his influence to tamper with the jury; it was a matter of 'find Coll innocent or else'. Vincent walked free and the jury avoided harm.(2)

Clearly guilty, Vincent showed no remorse; in fact, he now felt invincible and was soon out of control. He believed that money and intimidation made gangsters like him untouchable.

Seeking money to fund his increasingly extravagant lifestyle, Coll began operating on his own and robbed the Sheffield Farms dairy in the Bronx of $17,000 without Schultz's authorisation or permission.

## VINCENT GOES TO WAR WITH DUTCH SHULTZ

When the two men next met, Schultz reminded Coll he could only operate with his approval.

Coll told Schultz that it was his methods that had helped build his empire and rather than apologise, he demanded to be made his partner. Shultz refused and a rift developed between the men who had once been close friends.

While Coll was a violent man, Shultz was on a different level of viciousness and not a man to be crossed. Vincent had made a strategic error, and a paranoid and ruthless enemy.

Coll was now a marked and isolated figure and the final break with Schultz came in January 1931. Vincent was arrested and despite their animosity, Schultz put up the bail money. This was a surprising but clever move. Shultz did not want Vincent giving the authorities any information on his activities and despite his loathing for Coll he'd rather pay up than have him behind bars.

Vincent did not attend his trial which meant the bail money was forfeited. Shultz demanded Coll pay him back, but Vincent refused. This was the final breakdown in an already fractious relationship and the two men went to war.

Coll left the Shultz operation and proceeded to take a dozen members of the Schultz gang to join him in this new criminal enterprise. Coll's new gang and Schultz's mob engaged in a bloody battle.(3)

To finance his war against Shultz, Coll's gang began to kidnap rival gangsters and hold them for ransom.   This was a side-line Coll found highly lucrative and he was particularly good at it. As the war dragged on Shultz was terrified by the savagery of Coll's attack on his organisation. He felt Coll was reckless and his destructive nature was bad for business.

Coll was determined to drive Shultz out of New York. He began by hijacking Schultz's beer trucks and would then sell the beer at discounted rates to bar owners. He then burned down a warehouse belonging to Shultz, destroying a vast quantity of bootleg beer.

Coll cranked up the violence and he and his gang assassinated several of Shultz's closest associates and even tried unsuccessfully to murder Schultz. Vincent had to be stopped and Dutch Shultz retaliated in May 1931 when he arranged for the murder of Vincent's brother Peter his right-hand man and a fearsome gangster in his own right. Coll's tactics so terrified Schultz that he also offered a large sum of money to several policemen to murder Coll.

Such was Vincent's reputation that they turned down the offer.

Distraught at the murder of his brother Peter, Coll responded with a maelstrom of violence in the following three weeks he personally murdered four of Schultz's men. Despite the rising body count, the war was a stalemate and finally petered out into an uneasy truce, but both men would not forget or forgive. It was peace, but only for now.(4)

## VINCENT EXPANDS HIS TERRITORY

Despite the stalemate, Vincent Coll did manage to bully his way into the control of some sections of Harlem and the Bronx that were previously controlled by Shultz.

He soon owned a number of bars, not by purchasing them but by telling the previous owners they would be killed if they did not leave New York. Given Vincent's reputation and track record, most left. Vincent was fast becoming a major player in the New York criminal landscape.

However, he was also becoming an inconvenience for the New York criminal fraternity. Violence was part of everyday life but only if it was good for business and, for many, Vincent was bad for profits.

Coll also had no friends in the underworld due to his ongoing lucrative side-line of kidnapping other gangsters and holding them for ransom.

Whilst undoubtedly violent and volatile, Coll was no fool. He knew his victims would not report their kidnappings because of the underworld's code of silence. Also, any freed gangster would have a hard time explaining to the police authorities or the tax man where the ransom money that they paid had come from.

However, it wasn't just gangsters he kidnapped; Vincent and his gang began to diversify and started to kidnap showbusiness stars and successful businessmen.

They began with showbusiness legend, Rudy Vallée, and he received $100,000 for the singer's release. Next to be taken was Sherman Billingsly, owner of the Stork Club, the most famous restaurant in New York, whose family paid Coll $25,000 for his release. Then Billy Warren, a New York banker, parted with $83,000 to gain his freedom.

As Coll and his gang spread bribery money around liberally the police did not interfere with his kidnapping operation.

Coll then had the nerve to kidnap George De Mange, a close aide to Irish mob boss and his old friend Owney Madden and forced Madden to pay $38,500 for his release. This was a grave insult to his fellow Irish mobster and one he would eventually avenge.(5)

There were many other kidnappings that received no publicity, but all of them added to the growing wealth of Coll, who was making more money from this activity than he made in his war with Shultz.

But this enterprise was not generating any publicity for the gang in the newspapers. Coll was a vain man who craved the notoriety of Owney Madden and Dutch Shultz. He was frustrated that his terror tactics were not making him a superstar in the New York night clubs.

What Vincent failed to realise was that his fellow mobsters would pay journalists to promote them in a positive light. Coll's criminal activities, whilst newsworthy, didn't generate any feelings of respect or adulation.

This is not to say that Vincent didn't try to develop his image as a gangster; he was intelligent and handsome and spent a fortune on suits and hats.

However, he and his gang were so feared for their brutality that no matter how well they dressed, everyone thought of them as common criminals. When he visited the famous clubs of New York he desperately wanted the kind of respect that Owney Madden received, or that given to leading mafia mobsters like Lucky Luciano.

However, it was obvious to him that the club owners reacted with fear, not respect. He knew they saw him as a vicious young thug who was extremely dangerous or who might even kidnap them.

## VINCENT SHUNNED BY HIS FELLOW IRISH

Above all, Coll wanted respect from his fellow Irishmen, but this was not forthcoming. He was once deeply humiliated at an Irish fundraiser in Brooklyn.

A dance had been organised by fellow Donegal immigrants for a Gweedore family who had lost everything in a recent fire.

Vincent went along with his girlfriend and future

fiancée, Lottie Kreisberger. They entered the dance hall in designer clothes, looking every inch the successful couple. And they wanted everyone to know about it.

Vincent had lost touch with many other Donegal immigrants as his criminal career took off and this was the first time many of them had seen this infamous gangster. They didn't hold him in awe but in fear. Vincent may have thought he was a celebrity but to these Irish men and women trying to make a living in America, he was nothing but a violent and notorious killer.(6)

Vincent was taken aback by their reaction to him, no one approached him to give him a friendly greeting and everyone he talked to was aloof and did not hide their fear and distrust. It was plain Vincent was not welcome, even amongst his own people.

There were several of Coll's second cousins present and they were so embarrassed by his presence that they left the venue without identifying themselves.

Vincent was shocked and hurt. He had seen how the Irish respected Owney Madden and his gang and for the first time it was clear to him that he was not respected in the Irish community in New York.

Despite all his wealth, designer clothes and beautiful girlfriend, it was clear that his fellow Donegal immigrants despised him. The Gweedore immigrants had left Ireland to escape poverty, they had journeyed across the Atlantic to America to try and find a better life for them and their children. Through hard work, many of them were already sending their children to college and some had bought their own homes. They wanted to make America their home and believed that law and order was essential for them to do so.

The brutal lifestyle of Coll and his gang was, to them, a menace to decent people and a threat to the integration of the Irish into American society.

Many were also embarrassed and angry that the press had labelled Coll as the 'Gangster from Gweedore.' This they viewed as an insult to not only them, but their parish back in Ireland.

That night highlighted to Coll he was not welcome among the Donegal Irish and he would limit his contact with them from then on.

A hurt and embarrassed Coll would put a different spin on his visit to Brooklyn when he talked about it later. He described the Gweedore people as: "Little nobodies who were jealous of his success."(7)

## VINCENT THE CHILD KILLER

He also stated that they lacked ambition and were willing to settle for little weekly salaries instead of reaching for the stars as he had. He also said they were cowards who were afraid of the police.

Perhaps still angry from this perceived slight, Vincent

restarted the war with Dutch Shultz. On July 28th, 1931, Coll attempted to kidnap Joey Rao, a major Schultz lieutenant.

The attempt failed and in the ensuing gun battle on a public street, a five-year-old child, Michael Vengalli, was killed and several other children wounded.

The enraged media, shocked by the brutality of the incident, dubbed Coll a "baby killer" and filled the pages of the newspapers every day with negative coverage of him. The media called him the worst criminal in America, and the FBI named him as #1 on its famed 'Ten Most Wanted List'.

New York Mayor Jimmy Walker, the son of an Irish immigrant, christened Coll a 'Mad Dog' and the nickname made for great headlines, and it stuck to this day.

While on the run, the newly christened 'Mad Dog Coll' approached another notorious Irish gangster, Jack 'Legs' Diamond, and tried to form an alliance with him.

Perhaps fearing the noose was tightening around him in New York, he proposed a joint venture with Diamond to smuggle beer and whiskey into other states far from New York City.

Coll told Diamond they could make a fortune. however, Diamond was cautious in his dealings with Coll, and he had every reason to be since he knew Coll had once accepted a Mafia contract to assassinate him!(8)

However, before the new partnership could be

created, New York State police captured most of the Coll gang, and a few days later Coll himself and Legs Diamond were captured, and Vincent was charged with capital murder of the five-year old boy in New York.

The general consensus was that Coll would be found guilty and sentenced to death. The press speculated that Mad Dog Coll had an urgent appointment with the electric chair.

Mayor Walker, ever conscious of public opinion, was making it clear he wanted a quick trial, a guilty verdict and an execution to quell the massive public anger at Vincent.

However, this was not to be because Coll was acquitted in a bizarre trial.

## VINCENT ON TRIAL FOR MURDER

Vincent's lawyer was the famous defense attorney, Samuel Leibowitz, much used by the gangster fraternity and for good reason.

Leibowitz was the most successful criminal lawyer of his generation and the go-to man whenever a major criminal figure needed a defense attorney. He was a frustrated actor, and the court room became his stage where his oratorical skills and flair for the dramatic made him a formidable opponent for any prosecutor.

Despite his showmanship, the real reason for

Leibowitz's successful track record was his preparation — he left nothing to chance. Throughout the 1920s Leibowitz defended a who's who of criminal history and usually got them off.

During the trial Leibowitz used every trick in his formidable arsenal to select a jury he felt was as sympathetic as possible to Vincent. The turning point in the trial was focused on the key prosecution witness George Brecht. Leibowitz managed to destroy his credibility and that of the prosecution's, when it was revealed that Brecht made a covert living as a witness at criminal trials.

The trial was now a farce and the court room descended into uproar at this revelation. The prosecution case had collapsed, and the Judge was left with no choice but to allow Coll to walk free in December 1931.(9)

## VINCENT'S FATAL MISTAKE

Despite the let-off, Vincent did not learn his lesson. Even while awaiting trial, he embarked on what would be a costly mistake, the attempted murder of Charles 'Lucky' Luciano, one of the most powerful gangsters in America.

During the trial Vincent was hired by the New York 'Godfather,' Salvatore Maranzano, who despite being the most powerful mobster in the city, feared Luciano would kill him and take over. It seems paranoia was not just restricted to Dutch Schultz.

Despite the risks, Coll readily agreed to murder Luciano for $50,000, the highest amount yet offered for a single mob hit.

On September 10th, 1931, Maranzano invited Luciano to a meeting at his office to discuss re-drawing the mob map of New York. The real plan was for Coll to arrive later and kill Luciano during the meeting.(10)

Luciano, who had a wide network of informers, had learned of the plot against him and decided to act first. He sent his own men, who killed Maranzano before Coll turned up. While Luciano knew his life was in danger, he did not know the identity of the man Maranzano hired to kill him.

The fleeing assassins, however, saw Coll arriving and informed Luciano that he must be the intended hitman. This sealed Vincent's fate.

An enraged Luciano, while flattered at the high level of the bounty on his head, arranged for Coll's old friend from the Gophers, Owney Madden, now boss of the Irish criminal syndicate in Hell's Kitchen, to place a similar $50,000 bounty on Vincent Coll's head.(11)

Two violent hitmen, Leonard Scarnici and Anthony Fabrizzo, accepted Madden's bounty and the hunt for Coll began.

Vincent was again in hiding but, acting on a tip-off,

Scarnici and Fabrizzo burst into a Bronx apartment where they believed Coll was sleeping. They found six people there. Not knowing Vincent Coll by sight, they decided it was better to be safe than sorry and decided to shoot everyone anyway. In the ensuing bloodbath, three people died and three hung to life; but Vincent Coll was not amongst them.

Vincent was delayed elsewhere and arrived at the apartment after the shooting. The carnage was brutal and the shocked New York authorities informed the mob that this bloodshed had to end.

While the authorities often turned a blind eye to many criminal exploits in exchange for a kickback of the profits, the press publicity surrounding Mad Dog Coll and his associates was becoming politically damaging and even worse, bad for profits.

## THE MURDER OF MAD DOG COLL

Dutch Shultz and Madden also decided to act; this, after all, was getting bad for business.

A few days later, Coll received word that Madden, whom he trusted from his Gopher days, wanted to speak with him. Coll was informed Madden had worked out a settlement between all the gangs that would make everyone happy and save his life. Vincent had known

Madden all his life and trusted him, but this was to prove a fatal mistake.

A meeting was arranged in Hell's Kitchen where he would, ostensibly, be safe because the neighbourhood was under Madden's protection.

To avoid any further mistakes and to ensure Coll would now be recognised by his assassins, Dutch Schultz arranged for an old Coll associate, Abraham 'Bo' Weinberg, to work with the hitmen, Scarnici and Fabrizzo. Weinberg and Coll had worked together under Schultz, but Weinberg had stayed loyal to Shultz during the ensuing war between the men.

Vincent was now a desperate man. He was being hunted by every mob hitman in New York, all wanting the $50k bounty Luciano had placed on his head. On February 7th, 1932, Vincent checked into the Cornish Arms Hotel on 23rd Street.

The next day Coll entered the phone booth in the London Chemists drug store at 314 West 23rd Street at Eighth Avenue. He had been told by Owney Madden the previous day to call him to discuss the truce. Madden had set him up and Vincent had walked right into an ambush.

Weinberg identified Coll to the hitmen waiting in a car as Coll walked by and Scarnici and Fabrizzo stepped out to murder Vincent.

Only one assassin, Scarnici, entered the drug store, Fabrizzo and Weinberg waited on the sidewalk. Police reports later detailed that, as Scarnici passed cashier George Scott, who was waiting on a customer, a Dr Leo Katz, he turned to Scott and quietly said, "Keep cool now."(12)

Scarnici had a submachine gun hidden under his overcoat and as he approached the phone booth, he drew this and fired two bursts into Coll as he talked to Madden.

Taking no chances, Scarnici checked Coll was dead, then calmly replaced the gun under his coat and turned to walk out of the drug store. Passing the two witnesses Scott and Katz, he turned to them and raised a finger to his lips and made a 'Shhh' motion.(13)

He left the store and re-joined Weinberg and Fabrizzo and all three sped off into Eighth Avenue traffic. The hit on Vincent Coll had lasted less than 90 seconds.

The Coroner's report revealed that while a total of 15 bullets were removed from Coll's body at the morgue, it appeared that many more may have passed through him.

The New York Evening Post reported:

"How many shots were fired is not known. Some witnesses said fifteen others said fifty. As the killer backed out of the store, the door of the booth opened slowly and Coll's body pitched forward, three bullets in the head, three in the chest, and one in the abdomen and eight and the arms and legs."(14)

## THE AFTERMATH

The authorities never definitely identified Vincent 'Mad Dog' Coll's killers. Dutch Schultz's attorney, Dixie Davis, later claimed that gangster, Bo Weinberg, was the getaway driver of the limousine. Another suspect was one of Coll's own men, Edward Popke aka Fats McCarthy.

The submachine gun that killed Coll was found a year later in the possession of a Hell's Kitchen gunman named 'Tough' Tommy Protheroe, who used it during a 1933 saloon killing.

On May 16th, 1935, Protheroe and his girlfriend Elizabeth Connors were shot and killed by unknown gunmen in Queens. It is possible that this could have been revenge for the death of Vincent Coll.(15)

What we do know is that no one was ever arrested for Vincent Coll's death.

Despite a love of glamour, fashion and a deep-rooted need to be respected, Vincent was mourned only by Lottie Coll who, despite taking Vincent's name, was never officially married to Coll.

They had applied for a marriage license in New York City in January 1932 but Vincent's death less than a month later ended their marriage hopes. However, the press would always refer to her as the wife of Mad Dog Coll.(16)

Vincent was buried in St Raymond's cemetery in the Bronx. Dutch Schultz himself sent a wreath to Coll's funeral bearing a banner with the message, "From the boys."

So ended the violent and notorious life of Vincent 'Mad Dog' Coll at the age of just 23 years.

As is normally the case in mob hits, all three of the men involved in Vincent's death also met brutal ends.

Fabrizzo was murdered on November 20th, 1932, after a botched attempt on the life of another organised crime leader, Bugsy Siegel.

The gunman, Scarnici, was executed in the electric chair in Sing Sing prison for the 1933 murder of a police detective.

Bo Weinberg didn't receive much gratitude from Dutch Shultz for his part in the demise of Vincent Coll. Shultz arranged for him to disappear after discovering he was in league with Lucky Luciano to have him killed.

Dutch Shultz continued to operate his rackets for only a few more years. On October 23rd, 1935, he was killed at the Palace Chophouse in Newark, New Jersey, on orders from the new National Crime Syndicate headed by none other than Lucky Luciano.

As for Owney Madden, well, he left New York

shortly after the death of Vincent Coll knowing the end was in sight for the Irish mob and that the Italian mafia were now in the ascendancy.

**Sources:**

1. *New York Times, October 6, 1931*
2. *New York Times, October 5, 1931*
3. *"Schultz product of dry law era", New York Times, January 22, 1933*
4. *"Schultz product of dry law era", New York Times, January 22, 1933*
5. *New York Times, September 20, 1939*
6. *IrishCentral.com, February 2, 2020*
7. *IrishCentral.com, February 2, 2020*
8. *IrishCentral.com, February 2, 2020*
9. *New York Times, January 13, 1932*
10. *The Five Families, MacMillan, May 13, 2014*
11. *The Five Families, MacMillan, May 13, 2014*
12. *New York Times, February 8, 1932*
13. *New York Times, February 8, 1932*
14. *New York Times, February 8, 1932 15 IrishCentral.com, February 2, 2020 16 IrishCentral.com, February 2, 2020*

## CHAPTER 8

# THE MURDER OF NEEDLES FERRY—AL CAPONE'S CHRISTMAS REVENGE ON THE IRISH MOB

Between 1900 and 1925 a conflict raged along the New York harbours, a war between Irish and Italian gangs to control the lucrative rackets that were available along the busy and expanding waterfront wharfs and warehouses. This was the battle between the Italian Sicilian Black Hand Gang and a combination of Irish street gangs who would eventually become known as The White Hand Gang. This vicious conflict would come to a bloody conclusion on Christmas night 1925 at the Adonis Social club an Italian owned speakeasy in Brooklyn, when Al Capone settled his long-standing feud with the Irish Mob and murdered Cornelius 'Needles' Ferry from Gweedore. As a young man Al Capone had left New York for Chicago to escape the Irish White Hand Gang. Their power was so that a young Al Capone was sent to Chicago, as many sources confirm, because The White Hand Gang had him on a short list of those that needed to be killed.

The Mafia could not afford to lose one of its rising stars.

In reality, it was one of a few reasons for Capone's moving to Chicago, but it was certainly true that The White Hand Gang was as powerful, if not more powerful, than the Mafia in Brooklyn at the time and Capone was too hot a prospect for the Italians to risk.

Al Capone owed Frankie Yale a mafia leader a favour. Yale and his men had eliminated Al Capone's great Irish rival and leader of the North Dean O'Banion in Chicago on 10th November 1924. It was now time for Capone to repay his debt to Yale and to finally get his revenge on the Irish White Hand Gang.

## AL CAPONE RETURNS SEEKING VENGEANCE

Frankie Yale had already ordered the murder of Wild Bill Lovett the leader of the Irish White Hand Gang in November 1923. He was succeeded by his brother-in-law Richard 'Peg Leg' Lonergan who was an intelligent man with a hot temper and known as a ruthless killer. 'Peg leg' was so called because he had lost a leg in an accident with a train during a railway looting operation.

By the time the 22-year-old Lonergan took it over in late 1923, The White Hand Gang was a shell of what it was during it's heyday of the mid-late 1900's.

Peg Leg viciously began a fightback against Mafia encroachment. He was rabidly anti-Italian and would gleefully maim or kill any Mafia members trying to muscle in on his docklands territory. Woe betide anyone in his territory who would ever pay off the Mafia. He would often beat them up and then demand double tribute from the hapless victim. Frankie Yale one of the leaders of the Italian black handers and co-owner of the Adonis social club knew he had to act to stem the rising power of the Irish mob and asked his old friend Al Capone to repay the favour he had given him in killing O'Banion and to return and help him now eliminate Lonergan.

Al Capone had the perfect cover story, his son Albert "Sonny" Capone was suffering from a bacterial infection leading to inflammation of the mastoid bone located behind the ears. Capone and his wife Mae brought their son to see a specialist in New York.

On Christmas day 1925, as his son recovered from the operation which would leave him partially deaf, Capone's wife stayed with their son while he went to meet his friend Frankie Yale for a drink at his club. Capone and Yale had received a tip off that Lonergan and his key lieutenants were planning to visit the Adonis club as a show of strength and defiance.

The Adonis club was located at 154 20th Street in Brooklyn. It was a two-story building with a basement. A family of six also lived above the club in a small flat.

It was owned by Italian mobster Frankie Yale and amongst others boxing promoter Giacomo Stabile known as "Jack Stickem". The club was incorporated in 1917, with the aim of fostering positive relations between returning Italian and Irish soldiers and was popular with both the local Italian and Irish population.

Al Capone made his way to the club, a venue where he had ironically practised shooting as a young man in the basement which was a training venue for budding mafioso.

## CHRISTMAS CARNAGE AND REVENGE

Just after midnight an immaculately dressed, but heavily intoxicated Richard Lonergan entered through the open double doors to the dancing and dining room with his companions, Cornelius "Needles" Ferry a native of Gwee- dore in county Donegal , Aaron Harms, James Hart, Patrick "Happy" Maloney, and Joseph "Ragtime" Howard.

They were looking for trouble and began to make a lot of derogatory and racial comments to people in the club. As the night drew on Lonergan and his men became louder and drunker causing mayhem and throwing racial insults around while man handling women. They wanted to provoke a fight.

Witnesses later reported that as the jazz band played a lively tune in the background and the revellers enjoyed the party atmosphere the lights suddenly went out. The room then erupted into a scene of chaos and carnage as gunfire lit up the darkness. Tables were up turned, glasses smashed, and men and women screamed as they scrambled for the doorway in a mad dash to escape the scene.

Just as suddenly as the lights had gone out, the bullets stopped. As the lights went back on, they revealed a scene of carnage as Lonergan, and his men lay dead beneath banners that proclaimed Merry Christmas.

Peg Leg Lonergan died instantly without even having a chance to pull out his .38 pistol. His gun was found on him with all the rounds intact. He had been shot in his lungs and heart. He even had a fresh toothpick still dangling from his lips.

Aaron Harms lay next to Lonergan, he also died instantly without a chance to draw his gun.

Cornelius "Needles" Ferry was found dead outside in the gutter just outside the Adonis Club. His body had been dragged out into the street and was later found by a passing policeman Richard Morano.

James Hart was shot in the thigh and ear, but he managed to crawl outside the club and his unconscious body was found by patrolman Thomas McGrath and taken to Cumberland Street hospital. When he recovered consciousness, he denied all knowledge of a gunfight in the club and claimed to have been shot outside by an unknown assailant.

As for Maloney and Howard they managed to escape the carnage unhurt and immediately went in to hiding, until they were later arrested, but then released without charge.

## THE AFTERMATH

On December 27th, 1925, the police picked up ten suspects in connection with the homicide at the Adonis Social Club, including Al Capone, who admitted he was present but claimed to be sitting in as a doorman for the club that evening as a favour to the owners.

A number of other people were arrested in connection with the murders, although all of them were released eventually due to lack of evidence and witnesses. The family living above the club also claimed not to have heard any shooting!

In the end, no one was ever prosecuted for the murder of Lonergan, Harms and Ferry.

Frankie Yale had what he wanted, the Adonis Social

Club massacre eliminated Lonergan, and the White Hand Gang was in chaos. This allowed the Italian Mafia to eventually force them out and dominate the lucrative New York waterfront rackets. Al Capone returned to Chicago to see in the New Year, he was a happy man, he had taken his revenge on the Irish mob and murdered Needles Ferry.

# CHAPTER 9
## THE WIGGANS PATCH MASSACRE

E arly in the morning of December 10th, 1875, a large group of masked and armed men broke into the boarding house of elderly Irish immigrant Margaret O'Donnell in Wiggans Patch, Schuylkill County, Pennsylvania in the north-eastern United States of America.

Margaret O'Donnell had left Gweedore in County Donegal with her husband Manus to escape grinding poverty. Manus died in Dec 1867 aged 45. Now a widow Margaret ran a boarding house at 140 Main Street in Wiggans Patch, now called Boston Run, Schuylkill County, Pennsylvania.

Margaret lived with her sons James and Charles, her 20-year-old daughter Ellen and her husband Charles McAllister. Ellen was the mother of an infant son and was heavily pregnant.

The armed intruders were seeking vengeance against two alleged members of the 'Molly Maguires', a secret society based among Irish coalminers in the region, Margaret's sons, Charles and James.(1)

In the space of 20 minutes, Margaret would find herself pistol whipped, her son Charles riddled with bullets then set on fire and her heavily pregnant daughter Ellen McAllister murdered, shot in the stomach as she came to the aid of her mother and brother.

What could have caused such a savage attack on an unarmed family? The causes were to be found in the bitter and violent labour disputes between the Irish immigrant miners and the mine owners in that region.

## A TIME OF TURMOIL AND TOIL

It was a turbulent time in north-eastern Pennsylvania, with labour unrest in the anthracite coal mining region, where Irish immigrants toiled in dark and unsafe conditions.

Working life for the Irish emigrants in the mines of Pennsylvania in the 1870s was dangerous and exploitative. Many had escaped the famine that stalked their native land in the 1840s hoping for a better life in America. Sadly, for some they had exchanged hunger for the dangerous and poorly paid profession of coal mining.

Young and old laboured in the dark mines of Schuylkill county. Of the 22,500 miners almost a quarter where children and some as young as five were employed by the coal companies.(2)

While many of the miners and foremen were Welsh immigrants the vast majority of those who toiled, underground were unskilled labourers from the growing Irish population. By 1870 the Luzerne and Schuylkill counties had 38,075 Irish born residents and a large number of second generation Irish-Americans.(3)

Not only where working conditions unhealthy and unsafe, when the miners received their pay, it was soon taken from them in the 'company store.' Mine workers were forced to buy their weekly provisions from a store owned by the mine owners at a large mark up. It was not uncommon for workers to actually end up owing the company more money that they had been paid. This indebtedness tied them to the mine as virtual slaves.(4)

The Irish tried peaceful methods to improve conditions with the formation of a union named the "Workingmen's Benevolent Association." Despite some small improvements, the 'Great Panic' of 1873 (one of the worst depressions in American history) gave mine owners the perfect opportunity to further erode wages and conditions of the miners.

The mine bosses imposed a new contract framework

on the Irish mine workers and their colleagues which resulted in pay rates being reduced by as much as 20%.

The workers did not take this lying down however and in 1875 began a strike that lasted seven months. This was to ultimately end in failure after the Pennsylvania governor called in the troops to break the strike. Defeated and demoralised, the mine workers were forced back underground to work, accepting the new rates of pay. The union was irreparably damaged and faith in peaceful protest was lost.

The Molly Maguires society emerged from this background. They had originated in Ireland in the 1840s as a response to miserable working conditions and landlord evictions and were the latest in a long line of rural secret societies including the Whiteboys and Ribbonmen.

Many of the Irish immigrants who relocated to the Anthracite coal region of Pennsylvania originated from oppressed regions of Ireland where the Molly Maguires had fought for human rights. After peaceful methods had failed, in desperation they turned to violence to achieve fair working conditions and to fight back against the heavy-handed tactics of the mine owners.

Now operating in America, The Mollies were a secret society based among the Irish coal miners in the anthracite fields of northern Pennsylvania in the 1860s and 1870s. Thousands of miles away from their native

Ireland in the dark coal mines of Pennsylvania, rather than exploitative landlords, the new targets for the Molly Maguires were mine owners, company policemen and strike breakers.

Many of the Molly Maguires were also members of the Ancient Order of Hibernians (AOH), although not all members of the latter approved of the tactics of the 'Mollies', as they soon became known.

Intimidation, assaults and sometimes murder were employed by the Molly Maguires to rectify the grievances they felt could not be dealt with by a legal and political system that was hostile to immigrants and the working class. The 1870's were a period of great unrest in the Pennsylvanian coal mines.(5)

## THE MURDER OF SANGER AND UREN

The O'Donnell's were caught up in this turmoil as Charles and James were suspected of being members of the Molly Maguires. Along with Ellen's brother-in-law James McAllister they were the chief suspects in the murder of mine boss Thomas Sanger and miner William Uren on September 1st, 1875. This killing was widely thought to have been carried out by the Molly Maguires in revenge for Sanger's perceived ill treatment of mine workers.

Sanger had been foreman at Heaton's Colliery in

Raven Run near Girardville for three years and had a history of sacking Irish workers he suspected of being Molly Maguires.

He received a 'coffin notice' (a threatening letter with a picture of a coffin drawn on it) from the Molly Maguires in 1874 but had figured by this time the anger of his enemies was forgotten or appeased.

But this was not the case. He was gunned down as he walked along a busy street to work. Uren a miner and friend of Sanger, who boarded with his family, was also slain by the gunmen to eliminate him as a witness.

Robert Heaton, the proprietor of the colliery, bravely pursued the fleeing murderers and exchanged fire with them using his own revolver. No one was hit as the murderers fled up a mountain path and into thick woods to safety. Heaton organised a pursuing party and offered a $1,000 reward.(6)

## 'BLACKJACK' KEHOE

While there was no concrete evidence linking the O'Donnell's and McAllister to the murders, there was an obvious connection linking them to the Molly Maguires. Margaret O'Donnell's other daughter Mary Ann was married to Jack Kehoe an innkeeper who was widely known as the 'king' of the Molly Maguires.

Jack Kehoe, known best by his nickname "Blackjack",

was a charismatic Irish immigrant from County Wicklow. He had worked as a miner for several years after arrival in America before going into the tavern trade. An intelligent and gregarious man, he decided to move to the growing coal town of Girardville, were he opened a tavern and established himself as a well-liked and respected businessman.

Once settled in Girardville, Kehoe became its High Constable, which was an elected position with responsibility for keeping the peace, appointing other constables and ensuring the security of elections in their area.

Despite his position he did not forget those he had laboured alongside in the dark bowels underground. An active member of the Ancient Order of Hibernians, and a staunch supporter of the rights of coal miners, Kehoe earned the respect of the coal miners and resentment of the owners. He was an eloquent spokesperson for the union movement.

Kehoe's efforts to improve the lot of the Mine workers led to suspicions that he was the mastermind of the Molly Maguire activity in the area, and he earned the enmity of Franklin Gowen, the President of the Philadelphia and Reading Coal and Iron Company. Gowen disliked Kehoe's rallying of the miners toward unionisation. He tried to repress the miners' efforts in every way possible including slander and subterfuge.(7)

## THE PINKERTON DETECTIVE AGENCY

Franklin Gowen brought the mine owners together in the Anthracite Board of Trade and his response to the Mollies was to hire the Pinkerton Detective Agency to root out the Molly Maguires from the coal fields.

Pinkerton operative and Armagh native, James McParland was selected to infiltrate the Mollies and report back to the Pinkerton agency on their actions. Within a short time, McParland had successfully ingratiated himself with the Mollies. He observed and participated in several Molly Maguire operations. and even became secretary of the local AOH lodge.

McParland would eventually provide the evidence that would lead to the hanging of Jack Kehoe and 19 other Irishmen, executed in 1877 for membership and the alleged crimes of the Molly Maguires.(8)

## THE THIRST FOR REVENGE GROWS

However, back in late 1875, people now demanded justice for the murders of Sanger and Uren, McParland's reports would first impact on the O'Donnell's at Wiggans Patch who would pay a heavy price for their alleged membership of the Molly Maguires.

The mine owners using the Pinkerton Agency wanted to put a swift end to the Molly Maguires' attacks on their employees. The majority non-Irish population shocked by the murder of Sanger and Uren in their community also wanted the culprits brought to justice.

Anglo-Americans were either indifferent to the conditions under which the Irish lived or they were actively hostile towards the Irish presence in America. The Irish were stigmatised for being Roman Catholics and stereotyped as drunks and criminals. Yet, they were feared because many thought they would take political control of the region as they had in New York and Boston.(9)

The press also wanted vengeance and local newspapers were explicit in calling for vigilante committees. The Shenandoah Herald plainly stated that the institutions of the law were powerless against the Molly Maguires and that it was time to "take the law in our own hands and drive the men who are known to be at the bottom of the murders out of the district."(10)

The Pinkertons, using the information gathered from their agent, McParland, released a document listing the names, addresses, and AOH ranks of 31 suspects in various murders committed in 1875 by the Molly Maguires.

It stood as an open invitation for vigilantes to take the law into their own hands. The list included James O'Donnell, Charles O'Donnell, Thomas Munley, Charles McAllister, James McAllister and Mike Doyle as the suspected murderers of Sanger and Uren.

The list said the O'Donnell brothers and both Charles and James McAllister lived at Margaret O'Donnell's boarding house in Wiggans Patch, "a small mine patch near Mahanoy City."(11)

All the vigilantes had to do now was to decide when to strike.

One early historian of the Molly Maguires observed that, although the McAllister's and the O'Donnell's were suspected of the crime, "it was beginning to be believed that the guilty parties would entirely escape punishment."(12)

Vigilantes largely recruited from the ranks of the Silliman Guards, a local militia in Mahanoy City decided to act on the night of December 10th 1875. The Silliman Guards had previously been used before by the mine owners to enforce their will and break strikes in the minefields. They also acted without fear of arrest from the mine owner-controlled local police force.

## THE TRAGEDY UNFOLDS

In a tragicomic beginning to a terrible tragedy, the vigilantes became lost. Perhaps this was because it was a dark night or the Pinkertons had given incorrect directions. After knocking on a number of doors, the motley crew of would-be assassins finally received directions to the O'Donnell boarding house.(13)

It was a cold December night; Margaret O'Donnell was the last to go to bed. Before she went upstairs, she laid down a fire to keep the house warm and ensure her heavily pregnant daughter Ellen McAllister, who was due to give birth the next day was warm and comfortable.

At about 1am in the morning Ellen McAllister was awakened by a loud noise. It was as if a hoard of people were marching over the lawn. Ellen asked her husband Charles to investigate.

Suddenly the door of the boarding house was kicked in and around 30 well-armed and masked men flooded into the house banging on doors and firing their guns.

According to the later testimonies of witnesses, some wore oilcloth coats and carried lanterns to show them the way through the dark colliery town. Most wore masks to conceal their identities.(14)

The intruders began searching for their targets. Charles O'Donnell was first to be dragged from his bed. A group of the insurgents surrounded him and riddled his body with as many as 18 bullets. His body was taken outside and set on fire.(15)

The masked men knew who they had come for and soon James McAllister the brother of Charles another alleged Molly Maguire was dragged outside, and a noose was wound around his neck. He was hung from a tree in the garden and left for dead.

Miraculously he survived. He played dead and then wriggled free and ran for help to assist the O'Donnell's. The intruders could not find James O'Donnell who was not present that night.

Ellen, her infant son and husband Charles now barricaded themselves in their room, fearing for their lives. Thinking everyone else was dead, Charles McAllister fled out of a back window and bolted into the darkness, chased by some of the gunmen leaving his heavily pregnant wife and young son.

Some would say this was cowardice, but Charles later claimed he was going for help for his family as he was sure, as vicious as the masked men were, they would not harm a child and pregnant woman.

This was sadly a naive assumption as the masked men had already pistol-whipped Margaret O'Donnell into unconsciousness and were showing no mercy to anyone they felt was connected to the O'Donnell's or the Molly Maguire's.

Ellen though frightened and protecting her young son, could not bear the screams of her mother Margaret and left her room to plead with the assailants to stop. As she stood at the stop of the stairs, several of the intruders turned and looked at her.

One man raised his pistol and fired. The bullet hit Ellen in the stomach. Her eyes rolled in shock as she realised what had happened. Soon other intruders began firing at her. According to a later witness, Ellen's right hand covered the blood pouring from her wound while her left hand was raised to deflect the hail of bullets. Another bullet pierced her left breast.

"My baby, Oh dear God, my baby!" Ellen cried out, blood trickling from the corner of her mouth. She gasped, faltered, and clung to the stairs for a few seconds. But her strength quickly faded, and she crumpled to the ground.(16) One assailant was heard to admonish his compatriots: "We don't shoot women," but it was too late for Ellen.(17) This shocked the gunmen into silence and seeing what they had done they ran out of the door. Margaret O'Donnell lay unconscious but would soon recover.

In the following hours, Charles McAllister, and his wounded brother James made their way back to the house. The neighbours carefully lifted the burnt and lifeless body of Charles O'Donnell and brought him back into the house and laid him on the floor of the bedroom on the first floor. Above him, they placed Ellen McAllister, his sister, on the bed where she had slept peacefully with her husband and son just hours before.(18)

News of the murders spread quickly and soon became known as the Wiggans Patch Massacre.

## THE AFTERMATH

Ellen's body and that of her brother Charles, were taken to the nearby town of Tamaqua by train for the autopsy. They were then packed in ice and stored overnight in the train station storage pens to await burial in St Jerome's Cemetery.

The massacre shocked the region well used to violence between Molly Maguires and the mine owners.

While the police began searching for the murderers, numerous theories circulated as to the identity of the perpetrators of this heinous crime. The local Irish believed the ambush had been orchestrated by the coal and Iron police or even the mine boss hired Pinkertons Detective agency as revenge for the murders of Thomas Sanger and William Uren.

One lead did turn up just after the murders. Margaret O'Donnell grief stricken at the loss of her son, daughter and unborn grandchild eventually named the local butcher by the name of Frank Weinrich as the only intruder she recognised.

She could do this as she claimed that she saw Weinrich's face when she clawed at him and pulled down his mask as she fought back while he was pistol whipping her.(19)

This seemed a plausible accusation as Weinrich was

not only a butcher but the squadron leader of the Silliman Guards, a local militia in Mahanoy City.

As the police were controlled by the mine owners, it was no surprise that while Weinrich was questioned and held in custody for a short time he was soon released. It was rumoured a few other individuals were brought in for questioning, but no others were publicly named.

As the mine owners also controlled the local newspapers slanderous stories began to circulate denigrating the reputation of the O'Donnell's and even the slain Ellen McAllister.

The newspapers were especially cruel in their treatment of the victims at times, minimising the tragedy and blaming the murders on the Irish themselves, using the excuse that the vigilante activity sprang from a community angered over the acts of the Mollie Maguires.

One newspaper even labelled the O'Donnell's board house : "a place of resort for desperate characters" in which "all the parties implicated are doubtless of the very worse class ..."(20)

Margaret O'Donnell was the recipient of repeated and incessant questioning. At one point she simply could not take anymore, stating "I won't answer any more questions."(21)

A story began to circulate that perhaps the Molly Maguire leadership had ordered the murders as Charles and James O'Donnell had become liabilities to their cause.

This seems unlikely given the Molly Maguire leader was Jack Kehoe who was the brother-in-law of the unfortunate Charles O'Donnell and Ellen McAllister. Kehoe was a renowned family man, and it seems farfetched to think he would order the brutal murder of close family members.

It is far more likely that the killings were in retaliation for the alleged Molly Maguire murders of two local mine officials, however some historians now speculate that the attack may in part have been an attempt to smoke out Jack Kehoe and force him to commit an act for which he could be tried, and if possible, hanged. But Kehoe, was too savvy to take the bait.

What of the Pinkertons informer James McParland? Many claim he did take part in the attack, but that he was disgusted when Ellen McAllister was shot. Was it him who shouted, "we don't shoot women"? We will never know.

What is known is that after the massacre took place, McParland sent a letter to his superiors offering his resignation. He wrote to Benjamin Franklin of the Pinkerton office in Philadelphia, saying: "He was not 'going to be an accessory to the murder of women and children.'

Franklin immediately wrote a letter to Pinkerton:

'This morning I received a report from 'Mac' of which I sent you a copy, and in which he seems to be very much surprised at the shooting of these men; and he offers his resignation. I telegraphed 'Mac' to come here from Pottsville as I am anxious to satisfy him that we had nothing to do with what has taken place regarding these men. Of course, I do not want 'Mac' to resign.'(22)

In the end, McParland decided to see the assignment through. Which would end with the sham trial of Jack Kehoe and his fellow Molly Maguires.

## A SPIRIT CRYING OUT FOR JUSTICE DENIED

Nobody was ever charged for the murders of Ellen McAllister, her baby and her brother.

James O'Donnell fled to New York with his cousin Patrick O'Donnell and in fear of his life, he even changed his name and died in hiding.

As for the McAllister brothers, James fled the area never to return and Charles was arrested soon after and charged with the murders of Sangster and Uren. He was later released due to a lack of evidence.(23)

Margaret recovered from her ordeal, but not the heartache and for the rest of her life raised Ellen's young son and moved in with her daughter Mary, the later widow of Jack Kehoe.

For Ellen, her unborn child and Charles there was no justice. There were no trials. It also appears that for Ellen there was no eternal, peace.

The Boarding house was demolished in November 2006 as it was becoming dangerous, threatening to topple onto the adjacent roadway and power lines.

However, some believe that the spirit of Ellen McAllister roams modern day Boston run.

Despite the demolition it is still possible to see the cellar area and remnants of foundation walls. Members of the Pennsylvania Paranormal Research Team investigated the foundation area and declared it haunted.(24)

They claimed that they were approached by the spirit of a little boy who asked to go home with them. Who was the little boy? Was he the spirit of Ellen's unborn child? Or was the voice that of Ellen herself? Theories abound that the shock of the murderous raid, trapped Ellen's spirit at Wiggans Patch and that she pleads each night for the bullets to stop.

Whether or not one believes in ghosts, such stories show the emotional impact of the events of December 1875. Perhaps for some, Ellen McAllister cries out for justice denied for the Irish emigrant victims of the Wiggans Patch Massacre.

In 1979, Pennsylvania Governor Milton Shapp

granted a posthumous pardon to Jack Kehoe, hanged two years after the massacre. A 1970 movie titled The Molly Maguires, with Sean Connery playing Kehoe, undoubtedly helped to bring attention to Kehoe's cause. A pardon was granted with the support of the parole board and the district attorney who stated that the "trial was conducted in an atmosphere of religious, social, and ethnic tension." They stated the execution of Kehoe was "a miscarriage of justice."(25)

In another act of contrition, a commemorative plaque was placed-on the wall of the Schuylkill prison cell that held Kehoe all those years ago. It is an apology and admission by the Commonwealth of Pennsylvania that he and by association the Molly Maguires died not for guilt but for being Irish, Roman Catholic, and being pro-worker.

*Sources:*

1. *Shenandoah Herald (Shenandoah, PA), December 11, 1875*

2. *Melvyn Dubofsky, Industrialism and the American Worker 1865-1920 (Arlington Heights: Harlan Davidson, 1996)*

3. *www.feniangraves.net*

4. *Melvyn Dubofsky, Industrialism and the American Worker 1865-1920 (Arlington Heights: Harlan Davidson, 1996)*

5. *Kevin Kenny, Making Sense of the Molly Maguires (Oxford: Oxford University Press, 1998)*

6. *Kevin Kenny, Making Sense of the Molly Maguires (Oxford: Oxford University Press, 1998)*

7. *Kevin Kenny, Making Sense of the Molly Maguires (Oxford: Oxford University Press, 1998)*

8. *Kevin Kenny, Making Sense of the Molly Maguires (Oxford: Oxford University Press, 1998)*

9. *www.feniangraves.net*

10. *Shenandoah Herald, September 1875*

11. *Allan Pinkerton, The Molly Maguires*

12. *0 F.P. Dewees, The Molly Maguires: The Origin, Growth, and Character of the Organization (Philadelphia: J.B. Lippincott, 1877)*

13. *Shenandoah Herald (Shenandoah, PA), December 11, 1875*

14. *Shenandoah Herald (Shenandoah, PA), December 11, 1875*

15. *Shenandoah Herald (Shenandoah, PA), December 11, 1875*

16. *Shenandoah Herald (Shenandoah, PA), December 11, 1875*

17. *Shenandoah Herald (Shenandoah, PA), December 11, 1875*

18. *Shenandoah Herald (Shenandoah, PA), December 11, 1875*

19. *Shenandoah Herald (Shenandoah, PA), December 11, 1875*

20. *The Pottsville Standard, December 11, 1875 21 Shenandoah Herald (Shenandoah, PA), December 11, 1875*

21. *James D. Horan and Howard Swiggett, The Pinkerton Story (Putnam, 1951)*

22. *Kevin Kenny, Making Sense of the Molly Maguires (Oxford: Oxford University Press, 1998)*

23. *The Pennsylvania Paranormal Association, The PPA 25 Posthumous Pardons Granted in American History, Stephen Greenspan, PhD*

# CHAPTER 10
## PATRICK O'DONNELL

Patrick O'Donnell from the parish of Gaoth Dobhair in County Donegal was hanged at New Gate prison on the 17th of December 1883 for the murder of James Carey. Carey was the leader of a republican group called the Invincible's and his Queens evidence led to the hanging of five members of his group who were found guilty for what became known as the Phoenix Park murders.

Patrick O'Donnell was born in the Donegal townland of Min An Chladaigh on 1st September 1833. Little is known of his early life, but he was still a child when 'an Gorta Mór', the great famine, began in 1845.

Like so many of his fellow Irish men and women he was forced to flee Ireland as hunger and disease stalked the land.

## PATRICK IN AMERICA

Patrick left Donegal for America when he was 16 years old. His uncle Manus had emigrated with his family earlier and had settled in the anthracite coal mining region of Pennsylvania.

However, he did not go directly to his relatives. Like many of his fellow emigrants he found work on the east coast of America in Brooklyn New York and then Philadelphia. Trying his luck in Ohio he then moved to Canada, settling in Toronto. Despite his history of manual labour, he began to work in the hotel trade even at one stage becoming a butler.

This could explain why in later years people would assume his upright bearing was the result of military training, when in fact it was due to his time in domestic service.

He eventually re-joined his family in Schuylkill County, Pennsylvania. His uncle Manus had died in 1867 and his widow Margaret ran a boarding house with her sons James and Charles. Her daughter Erin and her husband Charles McAllister and young son also stayed with them.(1) Another of his cousins Mary Anne was married to Jack Kehoe, the alleged king of the Molly Maguires. His American cousins worked as miners and joined the Molly Maguires fighting for improved working conditions in the harsh environment of the

Pennsylvanian mines. The Molly Maguires were an Irish secret society named after anti-landlord activities in their native land.

They had originally formed in Ireland in the 1840s as a response to miserable working conditions and landlord evictions. They were the latest in a long line of rural secret societies including the Whiteboys and Ribbonmen.

In Pennsylvania many believed the Ancient Order of Hibernians (AOH) was the Molly Maguires' cover or working name, which was recognized by the state as a legitimate organisation. Once an Irishman had proven himself in the AOH, he could then be inducted into the Molly Maguires. When the AOH could not make changes through legislation, the Molly Maguires allegedly tried to make changes through force.(2)

The Molly Maguires in America, though not officially affiliated with Clan na Gael or any Fenian organisation, were also strong supporters of Irish independence. Patrick's family were key members of the Maguires and involved in some of the highest profile acts of sabotage in the struggle.

It was alleged that his cousins Charles and James had been involved in the murder of mine boss Thomas Sanger and miner William Uren on September 1st, 1875. This was widely known as having been conducted by the Molly Maguire's in revenge for Sangers perceived ill treatment of mine workers.(3)

Thomas Sanger, foreman of Heaton's Colliery in Raven Run near Girardville, and miner William Uren had been gunned down as they walked along an empty street to work. Sanger was targeted because of an alleged workplace grievance, while Uren, who boarded with the Sanger family, was slain to eliminate him as a witness.

The Mine owners had a determination to break the Maguires and brutal tactics including murder had not been uncommon from them.

On the night of 10th December 1875, a group of masked men attacked the O'Donnell boarding house and Patricks cousins Charles and Ellen died, in what was to become known as the Wiggans Patch Massacre.

Some members of the family escaped, including Patrick, and they resolved to retaliate against those involved in the maiming and murder of their friends and relations. This was not easy in a highly charged situation, and it was clear that Patrick O'Donnell was now in grave danger.

Kevin Kenny in his book 'Making sense of the Molly Maguire's' suggests it was at this stage that O'Donnell resolved to leave America and return to Ireland.(4)

Patrick first went to New York along with his cousin James who had escaped the attack on the boarding house. In New York Patrick heard of riches to be made in the diamond and gold mines in South Africa and decided to seek out a new life for himself. But first in

May 1883 Patrick left America to visit his mother and brother who still lived in Donegal.

## THE PHOENIX PARK MURDERS

As Patrick O'Donnell planned to return to his native Donegal, little did he know as he sat in New York that across the Atlantic ocean in Dublin, murders were about to be committed that would change his life forever and eventually enter his name into the annals of Irish history. The Ireland O'Donnell returned to was still reeling from the turbulent events of a year earlier when the Chief Secretary of Ireland, Lord Frederick Cavendish and the Permanent undersecretary Thomas Henry Burke had been assassinated in what had become known as the 'Phoenix Park murders'.

On a warm evening on the 6th of May 1882 Thomas Henry Burke, the most senior civil servant in Ireland decided to enjoy a walk through the Phoenix Park. He was unaware that assassins had decided he had to die, in the fightback against British rule in Ireland.

Burke had not been the original target, his assassins had originally intended to murder W.E Forster but he had recently resigned as Chief Secretary of Ireland, so Burke would have to do.

Burke was recognised as a hardworking and an efficient public servant, but he was also heavily involved in implementing what had been perceived as draconian action against the Land League during the first land war from 1879 onwards – especially the Coercion Act of 1881, which banned the Land League and under which its leaders were arrested.

Perhaps this was why he was targeted for assassination, but the ostensible reason was retaliation for the Royal Irish Constabulary opening fire on a protesting crowd at Ballina County Mayo.

The previous day the assassins had waited for Burke to enjoy his usual walk in Phoenix park, but he did not show, now they hoped for better luck.

As Burkes coach approached the Phoenix park it came upon Lord Frederick Cavendish, the newly appointed Chief Secretary for Ireland (who was married to the favourite niece of the British Liberal Prime Minister William Ewart Gladstone).

No stranger to Dublin Cavendish having met with officials in Dublin Castle immediately after his arrival in Dublin, had decided to walk to the Chief Secretary's Lodge in the Phoenix Park (now the residence of the US ambassador).

Burke asked Cavendish to join him on his daily walk, in what would turn out to be a fateful choice, Cavendish agreed.

As both men walked through the park they were attacked and stabbed by a man who killed them both with a hospital scalpel. In what became to be known as the Phoenix Park murders.

A republican group called the "Irish National Invincible's" claimed responsibility for the killings.

The group is usually referred to as the 'Invincible's' and grew as a splinter group of the Irish Republican Brotherhood (IRB). The IRB was a secret society dedicated to the overthrow of British rule in Ireland.

The Invincible's had been extremely active in Dublin between 1881 and 1883 with a plan to kill as many of the Dublin Castle establishment as possible.

The murder shook the British establishment to the very top, all the way to 10 Downing Street.

In 1864 Cavendish had married Mrs Gladstone's favourite niece, Lucy Lyttelton, and the young couple were part of the prime minister's inner family circle. Lucy was the daughter of the fourth Lord Lyttelton and his first wife, Mary (née Glynne), a sister of Mrs Gladstone.(6)

The Gladstone's had treated Lucy like a daughter when her mother died in 1857.

As Prime Minister Gladstone would have had a professional interest in ensuring the perpetrators were caught but for him this became a personal crusade to ensure that justice would be done at any cost.

Given the high profile of the murders, responsibility for the investigation was given to the British state's premier policeman in Ireland, Superintendent John Mallon who headed up the notorious and feared G Division of Dublin Castle.

A Roman Catholic from County Armagh, Mallon's 'G' division was a unit of plainclothes detectives who were often tasked with spying, recruitment of informers, prevention of political violence and apprehension of Irish republican political activists in the 19th century.

Dublin castle and the G men began hunting down the Invincible's.

The initial suspects were several fenian activists who had been recruited from abroad by leading members of the Land League. Mallon a shrewd and tenacious detective, began interrogating them gradually piecing together the conspiracy. This information led him to James Carey who was quickly arrested.

James Carey was a Dubliner who had started out as a brick layer before becoming a slum landlord. He had also been recently elected to the Dublin Corporation and was even spoken as a potential future mayor.

Careys fenian credentials were impeccable. He had been active in revolutionary circles as a member of the fenians since the 1860s. He had even taken part in the failed rebellion of 1867.

He had also been a leading member of the Irish Republican Brotherhood (IRB) rising to become its treasurer.

He left the IRB in 1881 following an argument on future strategy. Carey favoured a more direct approach to removing the British from Ireland and formed a new group called the Invincible's, who would claim responsibility for the Phoenix Park murders.

In his book 'Irish Conspiracies. Recollections of John Mallon', Detective Mallon said of Carey.

"He was the only one among the conspirators capable of addressing a meeting. He appreciated the importance of appearances too; he smoked cigars and wore kid gloves on the journeys from prison to the courthouse".(7)

Under pressure from Mallon and faced with a charge of murder and inevitable execution, James Carey chose to turn Queens's evidence and testify against his fellow conspirators.

Careys decision to betray his comrades had in part been made due to British subterfuge. James Carey had been led to believe wrongly that his close friend Daniel Curley was about to inform on him. Carey decided to do a deal first.

When Carey appeared for the prosecution in Court, shock ran through the Invincible's, each looking with disgust at him and shouting abuse, forcing intervention by the judges.

Carey was denounced as a scoundrel, a thief and a liar.(8) British retribution was swift, because of Carey's testimony eight men were sentenced to penal servitude while five men were condemned to die. Between May and June 1883, Joe Brady, Daniel Curley, Thomas Caffrey, Michael Fagan and Tim Kelly all hanged at Kilmainham jail.

What made Careys betrayal all the more poignant, was that one of the men his testimony condemned to die was Daniel Curley, who was the god father of his two-month-old child.

As for Carey he was now a problem for the British establishment. He had been given a pardon and a new identity, but he could not stay in Ireland. Other possible homes such as USA, Canada and Australia were ruled out due to the Fenian networks operating in them.

It was decided that Carey and his family would be given a new life in the Natal region of South Africa.

The British spirited away Carey's wife and their seven children and they were placed in a lodging house in the East End of London. As for Carey he was safe in Kilmainham Gaol waiting for the travel arrangements to be finalised.

Mrs Carey and five of the children were put aboard the ship Kinfauns Castle in London as steerage passengers and Carey now with the two eldest children joined the ship at Dartmouth, all of them travelling as family under the name of Power, Mrs Carey's maiden name, bound for Cape Town.(9)

Little did they know that a fellow passenger was

Patrick O'Donnell who was journeying to South Africa to forge a new life in the Diamond and Gold Mines of Natal.

## THE JOURNEY TO CAPE TOWN

O'Donnell and his cousin had returned from New York to visit his Mother in Gweedore. James returned to America, but Patrick had already decided to try his luck in the diamond mines of South Africa.

He first went to Derry then Liverpool and finally onto London where he met another Donegal native Susan Gallagher. Patrick proposed and suggested that Susan accompany him to make a new life in south Africa. They could not be married as O'Donnell already had a wife in America, they none the less booked passage on the Kinfauns Castle as Mr and Mrs Patrick O'Donnell.

On the long voyage James Carey or as he was now known 'James Power', kept his true identity a nervous secret. As the Kinfauns Castle made its way to Cape Town, it was no surprise that Patrick O'Donnell and James Carey mingled together. Witnesses later testified that they became friendly, played dice and cards and spent many nights drinking together.

At Cape Town before the passengers were transferred to a coastal steamer Melrose to complete the voyage to

Natal, the O'Donnells and the Carey family had time to go ashore.

Patrick O'Donnell and James Carey decided to go drinking and in a Cape Town Bar, it was there that James Carey's mask as James Power slipped.

As the drink took hold, Carey began singing Irish songs and ranting against English injustice. In a drunken rage he pulled out a revolver while arguing with English patrons and a brawl broke out.

Another passenger from the Kinfauns Castle by the name of Robert Cubitt was told by the angry bar owner that Powers true identity was James Carey. To back up his claim he produced a picture of Carey from the Dublin Weekly Freeman of 5th of May that covered the Invincibles trial and told of Carey turning Queens evidence.

Cubitt immediately showed the picture to O'Donnell who despite showing no anger or concern was heard to say: "I'll shoot him."(8)

Irish nationalists, both committed and otherwise, whether based in Ireland, America or elsewhere, were passionate in their denunciation of Carey. Was it this anger that provoked Patricks statement? Or was it guilt? O'Donnell had been a Molly Maguire; he had seen the injustices meted out by the mine owners and he had even witnessed members of his own family brutally murdered by hired killers.

Having failed to avenge them, was his reaction a

form of penance where he would seek retribution for his relatives and the five men hanged by Careys evidence and betrayal?

Carey had no idea his cover was blown but as the passengers embarked on the Melrose, rumour was rife in Cape Town that James Power was in fact James Carey the Invincible and traitor.

The Melrose left Cape Town on the 28th of July 1883, and it did not take long for Patrick O'Donnell to act.

## THE MURDER OF JAMES CAREY

On the afternoon of the 29th of July 1883, the Melrose was off the coast of Table Bay. Patrick O'Donnell and James Carey were playing cards and having a drink in the saloon bar.

Suddenly the card table was overturned, and shots rang out.

O'Donnell shot Carey first in the neck using a revolver he had smuggled aboard. As Carey staggered from the table and tried to flee, Patrick rose and shot Carey in the back. Hearing the commotion Mrs Carey entered the room and her husband fell into her arms. Another shot rang out and again hit him in the back. James Carey fell to the floor dead.

Patrick O'Donnell approached the distraught and

blood-stained Mrs Carey and offered her his hand and was reported to have said: "I'm sorry I had to do it."

However, others would claim later that he in fact said, "I'm sorry I was sent to do it."

It is worth noting that in any murder trial saying 'I was sent to do it' would imply a conspiracy, but I had to do it, whilst still an admission of guilt, would suggest a more personal motive.

As we will see, both versions were discussed at the trial of Patrick O'Donnell as the key planks of both the defence and prosecution cases. No matter what was said, James Carey was dead, and Patrick O'Donnell offered no resistance as he was arrested and placed in chains.

During a search of O'Donnell's cabin another revolver with a box of cartridges was found along with a picture of James Carey.

Patrick O'Donnell and the body of James Carey were taken ashore at Port Elisabeth. O'Donnell was brought before the magistrate and remanded for trial. James Carey was buried in the North End Graveyard in Port Elizabeth.

Amidst the tragedy of the murder two acts of kindness were offered to both O'Donnell and the remains of Carey. These came from a local Doctor Frederick Ensor, who was the district surgeon for Port Elizabeth and was integrally involved with the case. He conducted the autopsy on Carey and gave evidence at the subsequent enquiry.

Ensor also went to see Patrick O'Donnell and asked if he could help him in any way. O'Donnell asked him to take care of Susan Gallagher who was travelling with him as his wife. Dr Ensor reassured him he would ensure local clergy looked to her welfare. In later days, the Doctor would recall that O'Donnell became emotional and thanked him saying: "That's all I care for."(9)

Dr Ensor ensured O'Donnell began receiving a proper meal, as since his arrest, he was only receiving bread and water. His concern stretched to even prescribing a sleeping draught when he was told O'Donnell was not sleeping only pacing up and down his cell at night.

Dr Ensor also looked to care for the soul of James Carey ensuring he received a decent burial. The local catholic clergy had refused to provide a burial service for James Carey disgusted at his actions in Ireland. Dr Ensor decided he would say a few words over the grave of the deceased.

## THE AFTERMATH

In Ireland there was jubilation among the nationalist population. James Carey was a hated figure for his betrayal of his comrades and his death was celebrated throughout the land. An effigy of James Carey was burned in Cork and demonstrations in support of O'Donnell took place from Cobh in the South to Newry in the North.(10)

In England there was a strange reaction. The establishment were incredulous that Careys new identity had been so weak. After all he had only taken on his wife's maiden name, hardly a good cover story. Also, there was anger that the colonial authorities had failed to protect him.

Irish Nationalists began to rally towards the defence of O'Donnell. A fair trial fund was established in Dublin and appeals where made to the Irish in England. Irish men and women living in Bradford raised £4 10 shillings for the fund.(11)

In South Africa Patrick O'Donnell was hailed a hero by the Irish community and the sentries at the jail where he was held were continually pelted with stones by O'Donnell's sympathetic countrymen and women. The authorities feared a rescue attempt would be raised. In Cape Town prominent Irish citizens established a fund for O'Donnell's defence.

Over £30 was raised at a public meeting and O'Donnell's supporters approached Sir Thomas Upington, a leading politician and barrister to represent Patrick at his trial. This pro O'Donnell sentiment forced the British governments hand, who feared an acquittal or jail sentence rather than the death penalty. They pressurised the Cape authorities to return Patrick to England.

## THE TRIAL OF PATRICK O'DONNELL

O'Donnell's trial took place in London at the Old Bailey courts from 30th November to 1st December 1883. Again, the British Prime Minister Gladstone wished the case to have the highest profile and the Judge was one of the establishment's greatest supporters, Judge George Denham. The prosecution was led by the Attorney General Sir Henry James.

Patrick O'Donnell was hailed as a hero in America and a fighting fund for his defence was established by Patrick Ford in New York through his newspaper the Irish World. Similar fund raising was established in Chicago and Philadelphia.

These funds allowed O'Donnell to hire two leading barristers for his defence. A.M Sullivan and Sir Charles Russell MP who would later go on to become the Lord Chief Justice of England. The American fighting fund also hired a noted American lawyer, General Roger A Pryor to help defend O'Donnell and assist Russell.

Pryor who had been a general in the losing Confederate Army during the American Civil War was present in only an advisory role. This was because as he was not a member of the bar in the UK, he could not legally act on O'Donnell's behalf.

The prosecution had no proof that O'Donnell had been sent by the Invincible's or any other secret fenian organisation to murder Carey, their case instead rested on the testimony of a key witness Robert Cubitt, the man who had first told O'Donnell that Power was in fact Carey.

He testified that he had informed O'Donnell of Carey's true identity when he recognised him from an article in the 'Dublin Weekly Freeman'.

The court was shown a copy of this which had a portrait of Carey and a story on his involvement with the Invincibles. Cubitt told the court room he had shown O'Donnell this magazine and Patrick had then told him: "If it's Carey, then I'll shoot him."(12)

The fact a similar portrait of Carey was found among O'Donnell's possessions seemed to seal the case for the prosecution. This was further compounded when Carey's wife took the stand and, in her evidence, she claimed that O'Donnell had told her after the event "I was sent to do it."

The defence put forward an argument of self-defence. However, it was claimed that witnesses could only recall seeing one pistol, that in O'Donnell's possession. O'Donnell's defence counsel Charles Russell MP argued that given the nervous state of mind that Carey was in and that he was also continually fearful of exposure, he most certainly had a gun on his person at all times.

Russell's arguments for the defence lasted four hours and concluded with the assertion that Carey did produce a pistol and that this very pistol had been found in his sons' procession when police arrived.

It was to no avail, the Jury deliberated for only two hours and at 9pm on the 1st of December Patrick O'Donnell was found guilty of the murder of James Carey and sentenced to death by hanging.


## THE EXECUTION OF PATRICK O'DONNELL

Given the high profile of the case several pleas were made for clemency including from the writer Victor Hugo. O'Donnell's estranged wife travelled from America to plead his case but arrived after the sentence had been pronounced.

Fourteen Irish American Democratic Congressmen lobbied the American President Chester A Arthur, who officially petitioned on behalf of O'Donnell, once it was determined he had acquired American citizenship. The British government rejected this plea for clemency, and it was denied.

Patrick O'Donnell was executed on the 17th of December 1883 Hanged at Newgate prison.

Though buried in London, a poignant ceremony later

took place in his native Gweedore. On the 22nd of January 1884, a mass was held to repose the soul of Patrick O'Donnell. An empty coffin was then interned in the O'Donnell family plot and his coffin bore the inscription: "Sacred to the memory of Patrick O'Donnell, executed at London 17 December 1883".

In New York, an Irish Republican ladies group arranged for a memorial to be erected in Glasnevin cemetery. It reads:

"In Memory of Patrick O'Donnell. Who heroically gave up his life for Ireland in London, England 17 December 1883. Not tears but prayers for the dead who died for Ireland".

A plaque commemorating O'Donnell's execution stands at his birthplace, Mín an Chladaigh in the parish of Gaoth Dobhair.

A monument to Patrick O'Donnell in Derrybeg was unveiled in 1956 by Cormac Breslin TD. A Celtic cross stands beside Pete's Bar in Gweedore on the N56, its inscription reads as follows:

*I ndíl chuimhe ar Phádraig Ó Domhnaill as paróiste Ghaoth Dobhair a cuireadh chun báis i bpríosún Newgate i Londain ar an 17 Nollaig 1883 de thairbhe a ard dhílseachta d'Éirinn,*

Which translates as:

In memory of Patrick O'Donnell from the parish of Gweedore who was put to death in Newgate Prison in London on 17 December 1883 because of his high loyalty to Ireland.

It may be 137 years since Patrick O'Donnell was executed but his fascinating story and his memory are still remembered in his native Gweedore.

## Sources:

1. *Wiggans Patch Massacre, IrishCentral.com*
2. *The Legend of the Molly Maguires by Matt Loy, supplemented by Matthew R Hengeveld*
3. *historicalcrimedetective.com/the-mollie-maguires/*
4. *Kevin Kenny 'Making sense of the Molly Maguires'*
5. *Lord Frederick Cavendish and the Phoenix Park murders of 1882, History Ireland, 2014*
6. *Irish Conspiracies, Recollections of John Mallon, 1910*
7. *L. McCracken, 'The death of the informer James Carey: A Fenian revenge killing?'*
8. *L. McCracken, 'The death of the informer James Carey: A Fenian revenge killing?'*

9. *L. McCracken, 'The death of the informer James Carey: A Fenian revenge killing?'*

10. *'Revenge of the Fenians – A jubilee in Ireland over Carey's murder', New York Times, August 2, 1883*

11. *L. McCracken, The Fate of an Infamous Informer, History Ireland, 2001*

12. *The Phoenix Murders: Conspiracy, Betrayal and Retribution, Senan Moloney, Dublin*

Gweedore gangster Vincent 'Mad Dog' Coll. *See Chapter 7*

**Black Jack Adair, master of Glenveagh.**
*See Chapter 12*

**Irish patriot Patrick O'Donnell.**
*See Chapter 10*

*St Mary's Church, Derrybeg. See Chapter 16*

Gweedore
natives.
*See Chapter 15*

Canon
McFadden, the
fighting priest
of Gweedore.
*See Chapter 2*

**Professor Arthur Kingsley Porter.** *See Chapter 13*

**James Duffy, VC.**
*See Chapter 17*

# CHAPTER 11

# BATTLE OF TORY ISLAND

The last battle of the United Irishman-led rebellion of 1798 was not fought, by Irishmen or even on an Irish battlefield, but at sea, off the stormy waters of Tory Island in a naval engagement between the French and British navies. History records this as the Battle of Tory Island.

It is sometimes also known as the Battle of Donegal, The Battle of Lough Swilly and even Warren's Action, but the British admiralty lists it as the battle of Tory Island. This was a naval action fought on the 12th of October 1798 just off the coast of Donegal in north-western Ireland. The battle contested an attempted French invasion of Donegal in support of the Irish Rebellion of 1798, with a French squadron under Jean-Baptiste-François Bompart facing a hastily assembled

Royal Navy blockade squadron under Sir John Borlase Warren.(1)

Bompart's force had been dispatched from Brest the month before with orders to reinforce a French army under General Jean Humbert which had landed two months earlier.

## TORY ISLAND THROUGH IRELAND'S HISTORY

Tory Island, or simply Tory (officially known by its Irish name Toraigh), lies in the wild Atlantic nine miles off the northwest coast of County Donegal.

It is a small island measuring just three miles in length and one mile across at its widest point. It is steeped in history, music, song, and dance with breath-taking views and is now a popular tourist destination.

Tory is mentioned numerous times in 'Lebor Gabála Érenn', which is the apocryphal history of Ireland. Tory Island was the site of Conand's Tower, the stronghold of the Fomorians, who were a group of deities who repre-sented the harmful or destructive powers of nature and were personifications of chaos, darkness, death, blight, and drought. They were also feared sea-pirates.

The most famous of these on Tory was the Fomorian king Balor of the evil eye, who imprisoned his beautiful daughter Ethniu in a tower built on Tor Mór, the island's highest point. This was to stop her from bearing a child, who was prophesied as being the only person who could kill Balor. This was to prove a futile exercise as Ethniu did indeed have a child, a son called Lugh, who as the prophecy foretold, eventually did kill his grandfather.

Whilst Tory had a long pagan tradition, a monastery was eventually founded on the island in the 6th century by St Colmcille.

This dominated life on the island until 1595, when it was destroyed and pillaged by English troops, waging a war of subjugation against local Gaelic chieftains. The monastery's bell tower is the largest structure to survive and was built in the 6th or 7th century.

In 1608, the Siege of Tory Island took place, this was one of the final incidents of the O'Doherty rebellion which began when Sir Cahir Rua O'Doherty, Lord of Inishowen, started an uprising against the Crown authorities in the west of Ulster. O'Doherty, a Gaelic chieftain, had been a long-standing supporter of the Crown, but having been angered at his treatment by local officials he launched an attack on Derry, burning the town. O'Doherty may have hoped to negotiate a settlement with the government, but, after his death in a skirmish at Kilmacrennan, the rebellion collapsed.(2)

A group led by Shane MacManus O'Donnell withdrew to Tory Island off the Donegal coast and occupied a castle, but it soon became obvious they could not hold out for long. The Governor of Ballyshannon, Sir Henry Folliott, landed on Tory and quickly surrounded the fugitives.

To avail himself of a device known as "Pelham's Pardon", the Constable of the castle, Sir Mulmory McSweeney, began to kill his fellow defenders intending to hand their severed heads over to the enemy. "Pelham's Pardon" was named after Sir William Pelham who was an English soldier and Lord Justice of Ireland who refused any "rebel" the right to surrender unless he had killed another suspected rebel of higher rank.

McSweeney killed three rebels, before he was stabbed to death and cut to pieces. His own killer was in turn struck down. Some of the survivors of the massacre were then pardoned.(3)

190 years later another rebellion was about to end in failure, that of the United Irishmen with the Battle of Tory Island, the last action in the struggle of the uprising of 1798.

## THE UNITED IRISHMEN REBELLION OF 1798

The rebellion of 1798 was led by the United Irishmen, a republican revolutionary group heavily influenced by the philosophy of the leaders of the American and French revolutions.

The United Irishmen were established in 1791, first in Belfast and then in Dublin. The membership of both societies was middle-class, but Presbyterians predominated in the Belfast society while the Dublin society was made up of Catholics and Protestants. The societies' main objectives were parliamentary reform (based on universal male suffrage and complete Catholic emancipation) and the elimination of British rule in Ireland.(4)

During 1795 an alliance between predominantly Presbyterian radicals and discontented sections of the working class organised the Society of United Irishmen along secret, non-sectarian, and military lines. Agrarian discontent was rife, and many of the Irish peasantry who had formed secret societies of their own now joined the new organisation. A large French expedition sailed for Ireland in 1796 under the command of General Lazare Hoche, together with one of the leaders of the United Irishman Theobald Wolfe Tone, who had gone to France at the beginning of the year to obtain help for an uprising. Storms scattered the fleet, and, though some ships reached Bantry Bay, no troops were landed.

By the spring of 1798, it appeared that Dublin Castle had been successful in its determined efforts to destroy the Society's capacity for insurrection. Many of its leaders were in prison, its organisation was in disarray, and there seemed no possibility of French assistance. Despite these difficulties, on the night of the 23rd/24th

May, as planned, the mail coaches leaving Dublin were seized - as a signal to those United Irishmen outside the capital that the time of the uprising had arrived.(5)

Only in eastern Ulster and Wexford was the rising widespread. The rebels in the north were defeated at Antrim and Ballinahinch. In Wexford, where the rebellion assumed a nakedly sectarian form among the Catholic rank and file, many Irish Protestants were killed and others forced to flee, sowing an enduring legacy of sectarian animosity that was compounded by the brutality with which the British put down the rebellion. The Wexford rebels defeated the government troops in some engagements but failed to take New Ross and Arklow.(6)

The British determined to smash the rebellion appointed General Cornwallis as Lord Lieutenant of Ireland and Commander in Chief of the Royal Irish Army. He is of course famous for surrendering to the American revolutionaries at York's Town, to effectively end the American war of Independence.

By the middle of June, large forces of government troops under General Lake were concentrated in Wexford, and the rebels were finally defeated at the battle of Vinegar Hill on June 21st ,1798.

On the 22nd of August, a full two months after the rebellion had all but petered out the French surprised the British by landing 1,000 troops under the command of

General Humbert at Kilcummin in County Mayo. Humbert was joined by 5,000 local troops and inflicted a humiliating defeat on the British force at Castlebar, which later became known as the 'Castlebar Races', such was the speed of the crown forces retreat.

There was now naked panic in the British ranks and a desperate Prime Minister William Pitt the Younger, despatched thousands of reinforcements to Ireland, swelling British forces there to 60,000.(7)

It soon became clear that the apparent signal victory at Castlebar was an empty triumph. On 8th September at Ballinamuck, County Longford, the French force, vastly outnumbered, laid down its arms. The French were treated as honoured prisoners of war, but many of those Irish auxiliaries who had bravely joined them were promptly massacred when Lord Cornwallis ordered the execution by lot of a number of Irish rebels.(8)

The rebellion looked to be finally over, defeat for the United Irishmen had seen between 10,000 and 25,000 rebels (including a high proportion of non-combatants), and around 600 soldiers killed. Also, large areas of Ireland had been effectively laid waste. However, the final battle of the 1798 rebellion was still to come.

## THE INVOLVEMENT OF FRANCE

France in 1798 was ruled by the 'Directory' that had governed the country since 1795, in the final stages of the French revolution. It came into power following the end of the National Convention and the excesses of the Reign of Terror and the Committee of Public Safety. It lasted until November of 1799 when it was overthrown by Napoleon Bonaparte.

The Directory consisted of an executive branch called the "Five Directors" and a legislative branch called the "Corps Legislatif."

The Corps Legislatif was divided into two houses. The Council of Five Hundred and the Council of Ancients. The Council of Five Hundred proposed new laws while the Council of Ancients voted on the laws proposed by the Five Hundred.

The Directory itself was ultimately controlled by Five Directors who were chosen by the Council of Ancients. They acted as the executive branch and were responsible for the day-to-day running of the country.(9)

As part of the coalition of European powers united against the French Republic and its ideals, Great Britain continued to aid French royalists seeking to destroy the republic. The Directory was continually looking for ways to counter the British threat to the Republic's very existence.

General Hoche, the French General who had successfully defeated the British financed royalist rebellion in Vendee in 1795, wished to lead an assault on the British mainland as revenge for the continued British opposition of the French regime.

Hoche was lobbied by Irish patriots including Wolf Tone, who convinced him that a more suitable invasion target would be Ireland. The proposal was that if the French could land a force in Ireland, then the British would be forced onto the defensive. Irish forces would then rise in revolt, and a sister state to the French Republic might be established.

It was Hoche who convinced the Directory to aid the Irish in their fight for independence, though he would die in 1797 and not witness the rebellion of 1798.(10)

Despite ending Humberts' campaign at the battle of of Ballinamuck in County Longford on the 8th of September, the British had been spooked by the ease at which the French had landed in Mayo. They decided to monitor the French fleet closely, to ensure no other French troops could aid the now crumbling rebellion.


## THE FRENCH SEND FURTHER AID

The French, unaware of Humbert's defeat, sent a small fleet of eight frigates led by the battleship Hoche and

3000 men under the command of Commodore Jean-Baptiste-François Bompart.

They were again accompanied by the leading Irish revolutionary figure and one of the founding members of the United Irishmen, Theobald Wolfe Tone. He was serving as a gunnery officer aboard the flagship of the fleet, the Hoche. The French fleet left Brest on the evening of the 16th of September. The plan was to land troops in Donegal to reinforce what they assumed to be a victorious Humbert, whom they hoped would now be sweeping through Connaught into Ulster.

The British Channel fleet was now on full alert to ensure no other French army would land by surprise in Ireland.

This meant that despite Bompart's fleet beginning their voyage under the cover of darkness, they were soon spotted by a British frigate squadron led by HMS Boadicea, captained by Richard Keats.

He quickly set two of his ships, the frigates the Ethalion and the Sylph to follow the French while he rendezvoused with the main body of the Channel fleet, commanded by Admiral Sir John Borlase Warren.

The French were chased for a week into the Atlantic Ocean until they managed to lose the British in stormy seas.

This extreme weather was to continue throughout the

campaign, damaging ships on both sides and it would have a decisive impact on the final battle.

The British soon sent a Naval Squadron under Admiral Warren to the Donegal coast in search of the French fleet now heavily damaged by rough seas.

## THE BATTLE OF TORY ISLAND BEGINS

The British finally caught up with the French off the Northwest of Donegal, on the morning of the 12th of October 1798. The French commander Bompart now found himself surrounded on all sides by a vastly superior British force and the Battle of Tory Island was about to begin. The French fleet tried to make a run for it and went under full sail, but the British were soon in hot pursuit and gaining ground. Bompart the French commander tried to distract the British by ordering the weather damaged frigate Résolue commanded by Captain Jean- Pierre Bargeau to be beached on Tory. The commander ignored the order, perhaps thinking capture was better than the danger of beaching on Tory in atrocious conditions.

In the morning Warren was still hard behind Bompart, whose ships were now sailing in two uneven lines. Warren's force was even more dispersed, with HMS Robust and HMS Magnanime 4 nautical miles (7.4 km) astern of the French and gaining fast, HMS Amelia and HMS Melampus shortly behind them and Warren's flagship HMS Canada with HMS Foudroyant under Captain Sir Thomas Byard, eight nautical miles (15km) from the enemy. The other British ships were scattered throughout this formation except HMS Anson, which was wallowing to the rear, far out of sight.(11)

Bompart asked Wolfe Tone if he would like to embark on one of the faster frigates and perhaps secure his freedom. Tone bravely refused and decided to stay and fight. Bompart now had no other option than to attack the British fleet head-on and hope that some of his fleet could punch a way through and escape the British guns, which were now bearing down on them. He formed his squadron into a battleline and turned westwards, waiting for Warren's signal for the attack.

However, the French faced a fine seaman in Admiral Warren, and he had his own plan of action prepared.

At 7.00 on the morning of 12th October, Admiral Warren ordered the British warship HMS Robust to head straight for the French flagship Hoche. Captain Edward Thornbrough of Robust obeyed immediately and closed with the French, firing into the French frigates Embuscade and Coquille as they passed, before closing on the Hoche and, at 08:50, beginning a bitter close-range artillery duel.

This clever manoeuvre created space for the British warships HMS Ethalion, Melampus and Amelia to concentrate fire on the Hoche, which was now isolated and vulnerable.

Meanwhile while the British ship HMS Magnanime engaged the French frigates Immortalité, Loire, and Beltone.(12)

## THE FRENCH SURRENDER

The Hoche was heavily storm damaged, having lost a topmast earlier. When the British realized just how severely damaged the Hoche was, they began to rain down a volley of shells.

Less than four hours after it had started the Battle of Tory Island was over when the Hoche surrendered at 10.50am. She was drifting low in the water and 270 of its crew were either dead or seriously injured.

The French ship Embuscade was the next to surrender, having been battered in the opening exchanges by Magnanime, and further damaged by long-range fire from Foudroyant during the pursuit.

Overhauled by several larger British ships, Captain de la Ronciére surrendered at 11:30 rather than allow his ship to be destroyed.

HMS Magnanime, suffering the effects of her engagement with the Hoche, took possession of Embuscade and continued to follow slowly behind the rest of the fleet, while HMS Robust, which had suffered severely in her duel with Hoche, remained alongside her French opponent to take possession of the enemy's flagship.

The remaining French ships began to flee however the direction of the wind, took them across the path of the straggling British ships, beginning with the HMS Foudroyant. Most of the frigates were able to outrun the British pursuers, but the French ship Bellone was less fortunate and a speculative shot from a British battleship detonated a case of grenades in one of her topmasts. This began a disastrous fire which was eventually brought under control, but at a significant cost in speed. She was soon closely attacked by Melampus and suffered further damage.

Nearby, the struggling Coquille surrendered after being outrun by the approaching HMS Canada. Admiral Warren ordered the slowly following HMS Magnanime to take possession.

HMS Ethalion took over pursuit of Bellone from Melampus, and for two hours maintained continuous fire on the French ship. Ethalion was faster than her quarry, and she slowly pulled parallel with Bellone during the afternoon but could not get close enough for a decisive blow. It took another two hours of pursuit before the battered Bellone eventually surrendered.(13)

Hoche apart, Bellone had suffered more casualties than any other ship present.

During the evening, the surviving French frigates

gradually pulled away from their pursuers and disappeared into the gathering night, leaving behind four of their squadron, including their flagship, as captives.(14)

Wolfe Tone's mission had failed, the French flagship and four Frigates had been captured, while the surviving French ships ran scattered around the Donegal coast trying to make to safety.

The prisoners were landed at Buncrana in Lough Swilly, which was used as a British naval base until the final surrender of the Treaty ports in 1938.

The final blow for the United Irishmen came with the arrest of Wolfe Tone who was recognized by Sir George Hill. Tone was identified dressed in a French adjutant-general's uniform in Lord Cavan's home in Letterkenny.

Tone was immediately arrested on charges of treason and sent to Dublin for trial. He was sentenced to death but mysteriously committed suicide before the sentence could be carried out.

## BATTLE OF TORY ISLAND – AFTERMATH

The remaining French ships desperately evaded the pursuing British naval squadron as they tried to reach the safety of French-controlled harbours. Of the six French vessels the British captured three and the others made it to safety. The losses at the Battle of Tory Island ensured that never again would the French attempt an invasion of Ireland.

One other impact of the 1798 rebellion was Prime Minister William Pitt's Act of Union, which abolished the Irish Parliament, Ireland being henceforth represented in the British Parliament at Westminster.

The victors of the Battle of Tory Island were well rewarded monetarily with the proceeds from selling the captured French ships. The French Flagship Hoche was renamed HMS Donegal.

The French frigate Coquille was intended for purchase but suffered a catastrophic ammunition explosion in December 1798, which killed 13 people and totally destroyed the vessel. The last two prizes, Résolue and Bellone, were deemed too old and damaged to be worthy of active service. They were, however, purchased by the Royal Navy to provide their captors with prize money, Bellone becoming HMS Proserpine and Résolue becoming HMS Resolue. Both ships served as harbour vessels for some years until they were broken up.(15)

Admiral Warren received the thanks of parliament, and many junior officers were promoted.

In 1847 the battle was among the naval engagements recognized by the clasp, "12th October 1798", attached to the Naval General Service Medal, awarded to all the surviving British participants of the Battle of Tory Island.(16)

The British victory in the Battle of Tory Island finally ended the United Irishman rebellion of 1798. The losses faced by the Irish forces during the rebellion coupled with the reprisals meted out by the British against anyone who had aided the uprising ensured that the flame of rebellion was dampened in Ireland for many years but never extinguished.

*Sources:*

1. *The Frigates, Leo Cooper, 1970*
2. *The Flight of the Earls, John McCavitt, Gill & MacMillan, 2002*
3. *The Flight of the Earls, John McCavitt, Gill & MacMillan, 2002*
4. *Irish History 1798, Britannia.com*
5. *The 1798 Rebellion, Professor Thomas Bartlett*
6. *War of Wars: The Epic Struggle Between Britain and France 1789–1815, Harvey R, London (2007)*
7. *War of Wars: The Epic Struggle Between Britain and France 1789–1815, Harvey R, London (2007)*
8. *Cornwallis: The Imperial Years, Franklin and Mary Wickwire, 1980*
9. *The French Invasion of Ireland in '98, Valerian Gribayedoff*
10. *Cassell's Battlefields of Britain & Ireland, Richard Brooks, 2005*

11. *Cassell's Battlefields of Britain & Ireland, Richard Brooks, 2005*

12. *The Biographical Memoir of Sir John Borlase Warren, Bart, K.B. Tracy, p. 286*

13. *Nelson Against Napoleon: From the Nile to Copenhagen, 1798–1801, Robert Gardiner*

14. *Nelson Against Napoleon: From the Nile to Copenhagen, 1798–1801, Robert Gardiner*

15. *Naval Warfare in the Age of Sail: War at Sea, 1756–1815, Bernard Ireland, 2000*

16. *The London Gazette, January 26, 1849*

# CHAPTER 12
# THE LIFE AND DEATH OF BLACK JACK ADAIR

I t is often said that everyone is well thought off when they die, but there is one man with links to Gweedore in Northwest Donegal, of whom that can never be said.

He was the Landlord 'Black' Jack Adair, the mastermind of the infamous Derryveagh Evictions.

John George Adair was born on the 3rd of March 1823 to landed gentry in modern day County Laois, which was then known as Queens County. The Adair's were a wealthy family, loyal to the crown and with a long tradition of serving the British in Ireland and abroad.

They had been landlords in Ireland since the 16th century when John's ancestor Colonel Robert Adair had been rewarded by King William for his help at the Battle of the Boyne. Robert Adair raised and led a regiment at the Boyne and had been given a knighthood and large tracts of land in Queens County. The Adair's also had a cousin who was a Baronet and a member of parliament.

Young Adair's family had land and money, his father had inherited sugar plantations in the West Indies, which funded a comfortable lifestyle.

The infant Adair known to his family and friends as Jack, had his career mapped out for him by his parents, who decided he too would serve the crown. So, after attending Trinity College in Dublin, Adair entered the British diplomatic service.

Those that knew Jack Adair thought this was a strange career choice, given his short temper and aloof personality. Many that met the young Adair, often commented that he did not hide his confidence or sense of self-importance. Whilst this was not uncommon in the scions of the Anglo-Irish landed gentry, it was hardly the smooth temperament required for international diplomacy.

Despite these reservations, Adair was posted to Florence. It was here he would develop a love for Italian architecture and garden design that would have a major influence over him in later life.

A young Adair enjoyed the social life that the cosmopolitan city of Florence offered a young and single carefree diplomat. He was soon mentored by a British financier living in the city called John Leland Maquay. It was rumoured, that Adair repaid Maquay's kindness by having an affair with his wife and even fathering a child with her.(1)

It is unclear whether Maquay knew or even approved of this liaison, but the child William was raised by John Maquay as his own son.

Despite enjoying the delights of Florence, Adair's fiery temper did not make international diplomacy an enjoyable career and he decided to leave the diplomatic service and try his hand at finance.

Encouraged by Maquay, Adair made for America in the 1850s settling in New York.

He founded a brokerage firm and soon made a fortune speculating in mortgage loans and real estate. Adair would later expand his business with an office in Denver Colorado. He choose this location because of his interest in buffalo hunting and the opportunities offered by the ever-expanding American west.

Now a wealthy young man, he returned to Ireland to set up another business venture. He decided to invest some of his profits in Donegal, where he began to buy up smaller holdings of land around the Derryveagh Mountains and Gartan to create a single large estate of 28,000 acres (110 km2).

This was named Glenveagh, after the local name for the general area, which translates as "glen of the birches". It was here, in 1861, that he would carve his name into infamy with what became known as the Derryveagh evictions.

## THE DERRYVEAGH EVICTIONS

Adair's relationship with his tenants did not start well, in 1860 he began hunting on land he had rented to tenants, in violation of the rental agreements.

When the tenants quite rightly objected, an arrogant and angry Adair threatened them with eviction.

Adair had a vision for Glenveagh, and this was based on his admiration for the Balmoral estate of Queen Victoria and the architecture he had seen in Florence. He wished to build a palatial castle, ornamental gardens, introduce commercial hunting and establish a working estate based on deer and sheep and not the needs of the native Irish tenant farmers.

Adair began to import sheep and employed two Shepherd's, Rankin and Murray from Scotland.

Understandably, neither shepherd was popular with the local tenants, who had seen their arable land now turned over to sheep farming. It was no surprise that dead sheep began to appear throughout the estate.

Murray was particularly disliked and was constantly bickering with the locals and had several drunken fights with some in local drinking dens.

In November 1860, Murray was reported missing by

his pregnant wife. It was not long until his lifeless, beaten and broken body was found in a remote ditch.

It was clear that he had been murdered and local farmers were suspected. Rumours quickly began to spread that Murray had been murdered by his fellow shepherd Rankin. Locals alleged that Rankin was having an affair with Murray's wife and that he moved into her bed on Murray's death. This was to prove unfounded as she was heavily pregnant at the time of Murray's disappearance and soon left for Scotland once her child was born, without Rankin.

Another rumour was that Adair had ordered Rankin to kill Murray, to allow him to blame the locals, again unfounded.(2)

Rankin was presumed innocent and was placed under police protection.

No matter the rumours, two things were soon clear.

Firstly, the local police had no idea who had murdered Murray the shepherd and secondly, the relationship between Adair and his tenants was now at a low point.

Sources are available that claim Adair, who was a justice of the peace at the time of the murder, was unhelpful to the Police, who complained of the poor support they received from Adair. One is quoted as saying in a letter:

"I spoke to Mr Adair on the 20th of November to provide us with fuel and light, which he declined to give us. He also refused to allow us to cut timber. We have to patrol the mountains during the day and return at night to a damp cold house, with our clothing wet, ourselves fatigued from cold and want of food, having no fire to cook our victuals or dry our clothing."(3)

Despite the investigation, no one was ever found guilty of the murder of the shepherd Murray and the unrest between landlord and his tenants continued to ferment. Adair now secretly began the plans to finally implement his grand vision for his Glenveagh estate.

On St Patrick's Day (17th March) 1861 Adair obtained a writ of Habere facias possessionem.

This document granted him the legal, if not the moral right to evict his tenants and take back possession of his land.

He now began to gather a group of policemen and thugs termed as 'Crowbar men', with experience in evictions. The role of the 'crowbar men', was to demolish the dwelling place once the inhabitants had been evicted. This ensured no one could return to the property.

On 8th April 1861, a force of 200 police, three sub officers, the resident magistrate, and the sub-sheriff of Donegal Samuel Crookshank left from Letterkenny to undertake their legal duties. They met with the 'Crowbar men' at Glenveagh.

The evictions began at Lough Barra, where a widow, Mrs Hanna McAward and her six daughters and one son were the first to suffer. The family were evicted from the house, and with them removed, the crowbar men made short work of demolishing it.

The Newspaper reports of the time detailed a harrowing scene in which 'the recently bereaved widow' and her family were frantic with despair.

"Throwing themselves on the ground, they became almost insensible, and bursting out in the old Irish wail". (4) The frightening convoy then went from house to house over the next three days through Magerashangan, Staghall, Claggan, Ardator and Castletown among other townlands.

Twenty-eight houses were levelled to the ground by the 'crowbar men'.

When the evictions were over, 44 families were impacted making a total of 244 people left homeless including 159 children. All too clear 11,600 acres of mountain and valley land.

In the aftermath of what would be called the Derryveagh evictions, 42 of those evicted ended up in the workhouse, the terrible last resort of the desperate and destitute.

The press coverage of the suffering of those evicted

ensured that their story was heard by Irishmen and women across the world. Money was raised to help them in Dublin and France.

The Australian Donegal Relief Committee was established to assist the emigration of the Glenveagh people to Australia. This was a charity organised in Sydney by a Donegal migrant named Michael O'Grady. He arranged for fares to be paid for anyone wishing to emigrate and for land to be purchased for them in Australia.

Over half of those evicted would eventually decide to immigrate to Australia.

On 18th January 1862, the Glenveagh families left Donegal to begin their journey.

150 sponsored passengers from Derryveagh boarded the Abyssinia to Sydney in April 1862. The journey took 114 days.

Once settled in Australia they established successful new lives for themselves and their descendants who continue to thrive in Australia.

The story of the evictions has been passed down the generations and they remember their ancestors who suffered one of the most infamous evictions in Irish history.

## THE MARRIAGE OF JACK AND CORNELIA

The story of Blackjack Adair does not end with the Derryveagh evictions or even in Donegal. His story has more twists and turns and continued across the Atlantic.

With the vision for his estate being implemented, Adair left Donegal to return to America to ensure his brokerage business was being run effectively.

A confirmed bachelor in his 40s it was a surprise too many, that at a ball in New York City he met Cornelia Wadsworth Ritchie, and began to romance the 32-year-old widow, who would become his future wife.

Cornelia Wadsworth was born in Philadelphia on April 6th, 1837, but grew up at Hartford House, the family estate over 50,000 acres of land near Geneseo, New York Her brother was U.S. Representative James Wolcott Wadsworth, and her sister was Elizabeth S. Wadsworth, who married Arthur Smith-Barry, 1st Baron Barrymore.

In 1855 the family left for a two-year sojourn in France and England. Soon after their return in 1857 Cornelia married Montgomery Ritchie, the grandson of Harrison Gray Otis, the third mayor of Boston.

They would go on to have two sons James Wadsworth Ritchie (1861–1924) and Arthur Montgomery Ritchie (1861–1909), who struggled with mental health and jumped to his death while a patient at Belmont Sanatorium.

Her Husband Montgomery joined her father, Major Gen. James S. Wadsworth, to fight for the Union in the Civil War.

Major General Wadsworth served with distinction at Gettysburg, but died in a Confederate field hospital on May 8th 1864, two days after falling wounded at the Battle of the Wilderness.

Montgomery Ritchie retrieved the general's body and brought it home to Geneseo, then returned to the front lines. Sadly, just weeks later Ritchie himself died of fever.

Cornelia was now a widow, left without a father or husband and two young children to bring up.

Two years later she attended a Republican Party reception in New York and met the 46-year-old Adair. It was undoubtedly a love match, and the pair were married a year later in 1867.

They honeymooned at Glenveagh, where Adair shared his vision of the estate. Cornelia fell in love with the area and the plans for the estate and work would soon begin on Glenveagh castle.

They spent their time between Ireland, England, and New York. Cornelia also became a naturalised British citizen.

Jack Adair disliked New York and when his brokerage firm began to fail in 1874, he encouraged

Cornelia to join him when he looked west for new investment opportunities.

## THE JA RANCH

The couple and their two sons headed west to Denver, where Adair would temporarily move his brokerage business to his Denver office.

In April 1874 on a guided buffalo hunt, In eastern Colorado, Cornelia wrote a journal of their trip and in it she described the beauty of the west which captivated her:

> "Camped at riverside, travelled by compass, shooting antelope. On the prairie every evening, one seemed to have slept in the same spot where we had rested the evening before, so exactly alike were our camps on the Platte.... On each side, as far as one could see, the yellow treeless prairie, like a great ocean with yellow waves, stretched away without a landmark of any sort, not even a bush or shrub, only the short yellow buffalo grass."(5)

Near Pueblo, they met Texas cattleman Charles Goodnight who would lead their lives in a whole new direction. Goodnight was an Illinois native and former Confederate Colonel. Despite Cornelia having lost both a father and husband in the civil war, Adair and his wife soon became firm friends with the gregarious Goodnight, who ten years previously had been involved in the famous "gather" of feral cattle that had been living wild across Texas during the civil war.

Goodnight was already a famous name in the west having driven cattle herds north to Colorado along what became known as the Goodnight-Loving trail (Oliver Loving being the other leader of the drive).(5)

He had then formed a partnership with the famous cattle baron John Chisum, taking his herds to Colorado to sell to the army. The railway was expanding, however, and Goodnight could clearly see that the days of the great cattle drives were coming to an end.

Goodnight became their guide on a buffalo hunt and he regaled the couple with stories of the Palo Duro country southeast of Amarillo, Texas.

He described land which was ideal for grazing cattle on the open range. The cattle had ample grass in summer and could over winter in mild conditions protected by canyon walls. The land also had flowing rivers as well as outstanding natural beauty.

Goodnight was not just passing time with his wealthy clients on the Buffalo hunt, he was trying to attract a partner to help him establish a cattle ranch in Palo Duro. Adair and his wife were intrigued and looking for investment opportunities, but they were not so stupid as to buy land they had not seen. They decided that they would travel with Goodnight and his wife to see the proposed ranch for themselves.

In May 1877, Charles and Mary Goodnight, the Adair's and four cowboys, 100 Durham bulls and four wagonloads of provisions set off for the Texas panhandle.

The journey took twelve days and was not without adventure. Local outlaws had heard of the wealthy investors from the east and decided to kidnap the Adair's. They even went so far as to have a hideout established to hold them prisoner. Goodnight who was a man with many friends heard rumours of the plot and arranged for an escort for the party from the US cavalry. The kidnappers decided to end their scheme and the danger was averted.

Adair's legendary ill temper hampered the trip as he fell out with the cowboys who resented his high-handed treatment of them.

Again, Goodnight came to the rescue intervening to ensure the cowboys did not beat up his potential partner. Goodnight would later reflect that sometimes he regretted not fighting Adair himself!(6)

In contrast, while Adair was making enemies Cornelia was making friends and enjoying the spectacular beauty of the west.

When the Adair's came to the Palo Duro, they

realised Goodnight was not exaggerating and they immediately realised the potential the land offered and decided to establish a cattle ranch.

It was Cornelia Adair who picked out the site for the ranch house and so it is her rather than Jack who can be regarded as the true founder of the ranch.

Goodnight and Jack now talked about how the ranch would be established and financed. Adair saw the enormous potential and was keen to invest. Adair proposed that he would provide two thirds of the capital and Goodnight the remainder. Adair offered Goodnight a shrewd deal.

He would borrow his one-third share at 10 percent interest from Adair. Goodnight would be the daily manager of the ranch and supply the starting cattle. He would also draw an annual salary of $2,500.(7)

It was Goodnight's suggestion that the ranch be named the "JA" for the initials of his financial partner, Jack Adair. Goodnight began buying up additional land around Palo Duro Canyon, making sure the tracts were good for grazing and had enough water.

The following year Goodnight drove the first JA herd north to the railhead at Dodge City, Kansas. By 1882 the ranch had grown to 93,000 acres and had realized a profit of $512,000.

In its peak year in 1883, the ranch encompassed 1,335,000 acres (5,400 square kilometres) in portions of six Texas counties and boasted 100,000 head of cattle.(8) Jack only visited the ranch three times in his life, his real love was his estate in Donegal, and he began to use the profits he had made in Texas to make his dream of a rival to Balmoral in the hills of Donegal a reality.

## GLENVEAGH CASTLE

The tragedy of the Derryveagh evictions had shocked Ireland but had allowed Jack Adair to begin the creation of his vision of an estate to rival Balmoral in Scotland.

Work began on the castle in 1867 initially by Jack but then in partnership with his wife Cornelia. The castle the couple wanted was designed by Adair's first cousin John Townsend Trench, a land agent with a flair for design but with no architectural training.

Despite this he also designed a concrete Gothic town hall and other improvements on the Earl of Carysfort's estate at Arklow, County Wicklow.

Jack Adair's plans for his estate did not lack ambition and Glenveagh castle was built imitating the style of earlier Irish Tower-houses adding an air of antiquity to the castle.

The building stone chosen was granite, plentiful in Donegal but difficult to work and allowing for little detail.

His time in Florence as a diplomat influenced the

design of the gardens which were planted in both the Italian and French style, all with views of the glen.

The interior of the castle matched the grandeur of the exterior, he decorated it with sculptures both new and old, including sphinxes, figures of Greek Gods, busts in the Tunisian style and even two temple guardians taken from distant Bali.

The castle itself boasted a grandiose exterior, but a thoroughly modern interior.

With his dream home now built and with money to spend from the profit from his Texas ranch, Jack now turned to transforming the land around Glenveagh into the hunting and sheep estate he desired.

However, Jack Adair would not have the time to see his plans come to fruition. "Blackjack" as the locals called the hated landlord remained a loathed figure in Donegal. In 1884 the Edinburgh naturalist James Sconce reported that a woman from a family he had visited in Gartan had been overheard bargaining with a man to take her out to Tory Island where there was:

"… a stone which, if it could be turned, and the name of Mr Adair repeated over it, would have been sure to bring about his death within a year".(9)

This was the famed cursing stone of Tory Island, which according to folklore could bring death and destruction for anyone unlucky enough to face its wrath.

The woman was said to have died before she could make the trip, but perhaps someone made it in her honour. For the following year in 1885, while on one of his frequent trips to America, Jack Adair died.

After his last trip to the Palo Duro JA ranch, accompanied by his valet, Adair began the return trip to Ireland. He died of natural causes, age 62, while in St. Louis, Missouri.

## THE DEATH OF JACK ADAIR

Despite the rumours of fathering a child while on diplomatic service in Florence, Adair had no heirs other than Cornelia who inherited his entire estate including Glenveagh and the JA ranch.

Adair was buried in The Lea Church (Church of Ireland), Killenard, County Laois, Ireland, near Belgrove house, Belgrove, Ballybrittas, another one of his other residences, near where he was born.

The night before he was buried, a dead dog was thrown into his open grave. It was speculated this was done by disgruntled tenants.

In Glenveagh, his wife Cornelia had the face of a large rock inscribed with his name and the inscription "Brave, Just and Generous".

This did not last long!

There's a legend that lightning during a thunder-storm broke the rock into many pieces which fell into the nearby lake. I personally think human rather than divine intervention was responsible.

Two years after his death, Adair's property Belgrove House, which was an exceptionally large, country mansion was destroyed in a fire. To this day its ruined remains are called the 'burnt house'.

Cornelia would never remarry and spent the rest of her life living between England, Ireland, and America.

In America Cornelia inherited Jacks two-thirds share in the JA ranch. She worked well with Charles Good-night who continued as manager until 1888, when he decided to strike out on his own. Goodnight acquired the 140,000-acre (570km2) Quitaque Ranch with 20,000 head of cattle.(10)

From 1888 until her death, she was the sole owner of the ranch. Her son Jack had worked on the ranch in his early adulthood but ran afoul of Goodnight's strict work ethic. Goodnight demoted Jack after he caught him gambling and drinking with the cowboys.

Cornelia's heirs continue to run the JAs, which is the oldest privately owned cattle operation in the panhandle and was designated a national historic landmark in 1960.

In Ireland she built a Protestant church in honour of

Jack Adair near their Belgrove mansion prior to the destruction of the house.

At Glenveagh she set to work creating the hunting estate Adair had always envisioned. She introduced deer stalking in the 1890's. She continually sought to improve the castle's comforts and the beauty of its grounds, carrying out major improvements to the estate and laying out the gardens. Over the next 30 years she was to become a much-noted society hostess and continued to summer at the castle until 1916.

Unlike her husband, Cornelia was popular with the tenants and remained so until her death in September 1921.

She is buried near her husband in Killenard, County Laois, Ireland.

Cornelia is well remembered in both America and Ireland, while to this day the name 'Blackjack' Adair is said with scorn in Donegal and especially around Glenveagh where the name of "Black Jack" Adair, is forever a curse in the county of Donegal and the parish of Gweedore.

**Sources:**

1. *Culture, Carnality and Cash: The Florentine Adventures of John George Adair, published in 18th*

and 19th Century Social Perspectives History
Ireland November/ December, 2014, Volume 22

2. *Sin, Sheep and Scotsmen, John Adair and the Derryveagh Evictions 1861, W. E Vaughan, 1983*

3. *Letter from James McLain Constable to J McMahon County Inspector, December 26, 1860*

4. *Londonderry Standard, April 10, 1861*

5. *The No-Gun Man of Texas, Laura Vernon Hamner, 1935*

6. *W. T. Hagan, Charles Goodnight: Father of the Texas Panhandle, Norman, 2011*

7. *W. T. Hagan, Charles Goodnight: Father of the Texas Panhandle, Norman, 2011*

8. *http://www.jaranch.org/*

9. *Transactions of the Edinburgh Field Naturalists & Microscopical Society, 1902*

10. *W. T. Hagan, Charles Goodnight: Father of the Texas Panhandle, Norman, 2011*

# CHAPTER 13

# DID THE INDIANA JONES OF GLENVEAGH FAKE HIS OWN DEATH?

One of Donegal's most visited tourism sites is Glenveagh Castle, it was built between 1867 and 1873 by the infamous landlord Black Jack Adair and his wife Cornelia.

Its location is spectacular on the shore of Lough Veagh surrounded by lakes, glens and the Derryveagh mountain range.

Designed in a Scottish Baronial style influenced by Balmoral, it even has its own herd of red deer.

In 1861 Adair evicted 44 families from his land to make way for sheep and commercial deer hunting.

The shock and revulsion from those tenants that remained towards the evictions, led to rumours of a curse being placed on Adair and on Glenveagh Castle itself.

The curse was that no owner would ever have children and true or not, the fact is no owner had children from that point forward.

Adair died in 1885 and his wife Cornelia, an altogether kinder human being, inherited the castle. The hospitable Cornelia enjoyed entertaining, and the castle was even home to recuperating Belgian soldiers during WW1.

After Cornelia Adair's death in 1921, Glenveagh castle would endure a turbulent few years.

During the Irish civil war, the castle was garrisoned by both Pro and Anti Treaty forces.

Glenveagh was of no real strategic value, but each side craved the symbolism of holding the castle rather than utilising it during the civil war.

Once the Free State was founded, the Castle lay empty until 1929, when just before the world economy collapsed, a Yale educated professor of American art purchased the property.

This was, Professor Arthur Kingsley Porter an archaeologist, art historian, and medievalist who has been called a real-life Indiana Jones.

Whilst owning the Glenveagh castle and estate would give anyone an allure of fame, Kingsley Porter would be more infamous for his mysterious disappearance from Innisbofin Island in July 1933.

Did he fall from a cliff in a tragic accident, perhaps he killed himself, was he murdered or had the troubled man faked his own death and created a new life for himself in his beloved mainland Europe? This is his tale.

## BORN INTO WEALTH AND PRIVILEGE

Arthur Kingsley Porter was born in 1883, the third son in a wealthy family in Stamford Connecticut. Tragedy was soon to strike when his mother, Maria Louisa Hoyt died when Porter was only eight years old.

His father Timothy Hopkins Porter was a wealthy banker who suffered from regular bouts of depression and paranoia.

When his parents married in 1870 the union merged two of Connecticut's oldest and most influential families. Both the Hoyts and Porters claimed to have arrived in Connecticut in the early 1600s.

A young Porter was a classmate of John D Rockefeller Jnr at the prestigious Browning boys school in New York city.

Indeed, such was the wealth of the Porter family that an 18-year-old Arthur Kingsley Porter became an instant millionaire when his family trust fund matured.(1)

Porter graduated from Yale with a degree in law in 1902, but soon decided that the legal profession was not for him. In 1904 while touring Europe he experienced what he would later describe as a semi spiritual awaking. This happened in France while visiting Cathédrale Notre-Dame de Coutances, a Gothic Roman Catholic cathedral constructed from 1210 to 1274 in the town of Coutances, Normandy. In awe of the architecture and art on display, the 21-year-old Porter, now a wealthy man decided that he would now study Art History.(2)

On his return to America, he enrolled at Columbia University's School of Architecture.

## THE INDIANA JONES OF ARCHITECTURE

In 1907 Porter now gaining a reputation as a scholar of architecture met Lucy Byrant Wallace, seven years his senior, at a social gathering in New York.

While Porter was a handsome and shy man with a bookish nature, Lucy was a force of nature with a confident outlook on life and a busy social life.

Oddly suited to some, the couple however shared a passion for art and architecture and quickly fell in love. They married in 1908 and spent the next few years travelling throughout Europe, with Lucy acting as the Porters official photographer documenting his studies.

The couple returned to the US as the European continent fell into the horrors of the First World War.

As the conflict ravaged France and Belgium destroying much of the architecture, he loved, Porter returned to Yale in 1915 to take up a lecturing role, while he worked towards a Bachelor of Fine Arts.

In January 1916, he proposed giving the University $500,000 to set up a department of art history. Porter laid out the very specific purposes for which the money was to be used.

Yale frustrated by the strict rules laid down by Porter decided to decline the offer. Porter became disillusioned at Yale's lack of openness to having a full department dedicated to the study of the history of art and architecture. In 1918 Porter left Yale to lead architectural preservation efforts by the French government caused by war damage. He was the only American academic invited to join the commission.

He also became a guest lecturer at universities in France and Spain. His reputation was growing, and he was revolutionising the understanding of the chronology and diffusion of Romanesque sculpture.(3)

In 1925 the couple returned to America where Arthur became the chair of Art history at Harvard University. He was now at the top of his profession, and he became one of the founders of the College Art Association of America, and a prize in his honour is still given out each year.

Porters Wealth and growing reputation have led many to liken him to Indiana Jones. His personal finances allowed him to fund regular leaves of absence and equip his own expeditions to Europe in search of treasures.(4)

One such adventure involved the discovery of the sarcophagus commissioned by Count Pedro Ansùrez in 1093, for his young son Alfonso.

Porter was looking for evidence to back up his theory on the spread of Romanesque sculpture. He was convinced the sarcophagus proved this and he used his wealth to acquire it and take it back to America where he presented it as a gift to Harvard Universities Fogg Museum, where it was prominently displayed.

Scholars considered the lid of the sarcophagus was one of the finest examples of European sepulchral sculpture in existence from the Middle Ages. The discovery of the burial slab gave Kingsley the proof he had been searching for that Romanesque sculpture was practiced in Spain during the eleventh century. The sculptured style of decoration on the coffin lid was a divergence from tomb construction of the time. It contained large figures representing souls that had passed into the other world, Evangelists and Archangels, all in human form. The figures were depicted with large bulging eyes and the archangel Gabriel had long chiselled curls. Therefore, as an art object it was invaluable to archaeologists to further their knowledge of eleventh-century Romanesque Spanish sculpture.(5)

In 1931, Jacobo Fitz-James Stuart, the 17th Duke of

Alba, discovered the sarcophagus had been removed from Lèon and brought to Harvard by Porter. Outraged he lobbied the Spanish government, who became involved with the negotiations with Harvard for its return, but before any deal was reached, Alfonso XIII of Spain was overthrown by a revolution, and so the slab remained on display in America.

Negotiations resumed in 1933, and Porter consented for the sarcophagus lid to be returned to Léon and It was finally returned to its rightful place on the 8th of July 1933.(6)

## SUCCESS BUT DARK SECRETS

Despite his success porter was concealing a dark secret from his wife. After 17 years of married life Porter confessed to his wife that despite loving her deeply, he was gay.

Lucy Porter decided to stand by her husband, but this confession perhaps explains the scandal that clouded his departure from Harvard in 1929, where rumours persisted of Porter sexually harassing his male students. (7)

Porter like his father before him suffered from bouts of depression and his wife Lucy decided that a move to Ireland would help her husband recover. Porter already had a deep interest in Celtic history and art and the couple decided to purchase a home in Ireland.

Lucy hoped the change of scenery would ease her husbands troubled mind.

As 1929 drew to a close the couple purchased Glenveagh Castle and the surrounding estate for £5,000.

A recovering Porter now immersed himself in Celtic studies and he became friends with the Irish writer and artist George William Russell, whose paintings still hang on the walls of Glenveagh Castle.(8)

Porter also restored a fisherman's cottage on Inishboffin Island (Inish Bó Finne in Irish), which is located 3km from Machaire Rabhartaigh (Magheroarty) on the County Donegal coast. It was here that Porter began to learn the Irish language.

However, Porters Irish idyll began to unravel as his depression again began to take hold.

His wife arranged for Porter to see Dr Havelock, an unorthodox psychotherapist and sexologist in London. The Dr believed that Porters repressed sexuality was the cause of his depression.

He recommended that Porter give in to his desires with a young patient of his called Alan Campbell.

The bizarre situation took an even stranger twist when Porter's wife Lucy agreed with the Dr and the young Campbell became a regular visitor to Glenveagh

Castle and to the Porter's American home in Connecticut.

This strange relationship dynamic could not be sustained for long and when all three-set sail for Ireland on May 27th, 1933, Campbell ended the relationship and travelled onto London alone.

## DEATH OR DISAPPEARANCE?

Porter now relapsed into a deep depression.

Eleven days later, while spending a night at the fisherman's hut that he had lovingly restored on Inishboffin, Porter went out walking during a storm and was never seen again.

The inquest held that September, was the first in the short history of the Irish state to be held without a body.

During the inquest Porters widow detailed her frantic but futile six-hour search for her husband.

Lucy Porter gave evidence that she believed her husband must have slipped off the cliffs, fallen into the sea and been carried away.

It was also recorded that the next day she had told the author George William Russell that: "Kingsley will not return tonight, Kingsley will never return."

An interesting fact came to light when the inquest was told that one small boat had left the island the morning after Porters disappearance.

The inquest returned a verdict of death by misadventure, though privately the coroner voiced his opinion that Lucy knew more than she said in court. And that she acted as if her husband's disappearance was not unexpected.(9)

The inquest did not discuss Porters love affair with Alan Campbell , which had ended just before his disappearance.

As for Lucy, she returned to Glenveagh and funded research to study the "nature, cause and treatment of homosexuality". She also continued Porters archaeological studies.

Lucy sold Glenveagh to Henry McIlhenny a former student of Arthur Kingsley Porter's from Philadelphia. He had rented the castle each summer from 1933 onwards and in 1937 he purchased it outright. The estate was going to someone who shared Porter's love of architecture. In fact, McIlhenny had been a student of Porter's at Harvard. However. McIlhenny would fall foul of the Glenveagh curse and never sire an heir. In 1975 he sold the estate to the Office of Public Works which allowed the creation of Glenveagh National Park, and in 1983, Glenveagh Castle was bestowed to the nation, with the National Park opening to the public a year later and the castle in 1986.(10)

## DID PORTER ACTUALLY DIE THAT NIGHT?

The story of Arthur Kingsley Porter did not end with his inquest. A few years later, there were rumours of sightings of Porter in Europe, and these continued to be reported from locations all over the world for many years after his disappearance. But despite these stories no concrete evidence was ever found of Arthur Kingsley Porter.(11)

His wife Lucy returned to America and died on September 19, 1962, at her home in Cambridge, Massachusetts.

We will never know what happened to Arthur Kingsley Porter as his body was never found. Perhaps he died on Inishboffin, or had he faked it all to leave Northwest Donegal behind to live the life he always wanted to experience in Europe?

We shall never know.

There are some who perhaps of Porters slight similarity with Indiana Jones believe in a more supernatural reason for his disappearance.

That is linked to his disturbance of the tomb of the young Alfonso.at Sahagún in 1926. Could a medieval curse have been unleashed?

Perhaps a flight of fancy, but one interesting fact that is true, is that the sarcophagus lid that had enclosed the tomb of Alfonso Ansúrez in 1093 was finally returned to its rightful place on 8th July 1933 – the day of Porters disappearance!

*Sources:*

1. *Glenveagh Mystery: The Life, Work and Disappearance of Arthur Kingsley Porter, Lucy Costigan, Newbridge: Merrion, 2012*

2. *'The Scholar and the Studio: A. Kingsley Port and the Study of Medieval Architecture in the Decade Before the War', Linda Seidel, 1990*

3. *'The Scholar and the Studio: A. Kingsley Port and the Study of Medieval Architecture in the Decade Before the War', Linda Seidel, 1990*

4. *Glenveagh Mystery: The Life, Work and Disappearance of Arthur Kingsley Porter, Lucy Costigan, Newbridge: Merrion, 2012*

5. *Official Register of Harvard University Containing Report of the President of Harvard College and Reports of Departments for 1932, 1933, 31, 3. February 5, 1934, p. 309.*

6. *"Collections and Critiques | News | The Harvard Crimson". www.thecrimson.com, December 12, 1935*

7. *Glenveagh Mystery: The Life, Work and Disappearance of Arthur Kingsley Porter, Lucy Costigan, Newbridge: Merrion, 2012*

8. *'Glenveagh Castle – Cruelty, Cowboys and Celebrities', Daily Scribbling, June 15, 2014*

9. *Glenveagh Mystery: The Life, Work and Disappearance of Arthur Kingsley Porter, Lucy Costigan, Newbridge: Merrion, 2012*

10. *Castle History – Glenveagh National Park*

11. *Glenveagh Mystery: The Life, Work and Disappearance of Arthur Kingsley Porter, Lucy Costigan, Newbridge: Merrion, 2012*

## CHAPTER 14
# THE DONEGAL RAILWAY—
# TRAINS IN GWEEDORE

R ailways have played a significant part in the history of Ireland and the parish of Gweedore. The first railway in Ireland was planned in 1826 as a link between Limerick and Waterford.

However, planning was delayed and a railway line in Ireland would have to wait until 1834. This was the Dublin and Kingstown Railway (D&KR) between West-land Row in Dublin and Kingstown (Dún Laoghaire), a distance of 10 km (6 mi).

By its peak in 1920, the Irish Rail Network covered 3,500 miles or 4,200km.

Donegal would be well served by the Railway in part due to its proximity with Derry. The first lines in the county opened in 1863.

As the network grew, major towns in the county could be reached by rail, including Letterkenny, Burtonport and Glenties in the west of the county, and Killybegs and Ballyshannon in south Donegal.

On the Inishowen peninsula, a line went as far as Carndonagh.

In the north of the county, services were run by the Londonderry and Lough Swilly Railway Company, usually called 'The Swilly'.

The Londonderry and Lough Swilly Railway Company (The Swilly) was an Irish public transport and freight company that operated in parts of County Londonderry and County Donegal between 1853 and 2014.

It was Incorporated in June 1853, and once operated 99 miles of railway tracks. It began the transition to bus and road freight services in 1929. It closed its last railway line in July 1953 but continued to operate bus services under the name Lough Swilly Bus Company until April 2014.

'The Swilly' became the oldest railway company established in the Victorian era to continue trading as a commercial concern into the 21st century.

A small section of the network was originally broad gauge, but soon narrow gauge became the working norm across the county. The Donegal railways also ran to Derry city, which at one stage, had four railway stations. One in the docks area linked Derry with Letterkenny, Buncrana and the Inishowen peninsula, while the

Victoria Road station on the east bank of the Foyle provided a connection to Killybegs.

The Donegal rail network was a marvel of Irish ingenuity and at 225 miles long, it was the longest narrow-gauge system in Ireland.

The County Donegal network survived until 1947 without any major closures. This was due to the General Manager from 1910 to 1943, Henry Forbes, who introduced many economies, not least of which was diesel railcar operation for most passenger trains.

The station that serviced Gweedore was an important part of the Donegal railway and had a short but interesting history.

## GWEEDORE STATION

In February of 1891 a commission was established to examine the merits of two proposals to connect Letterkenny to the isolated areas of the Donegal Northwest.

The commission heard evidence on two suggested routes:

A direct line to Bunbeg via Churchill Creeslough, Dunfanaghy and Falcarragh

A coastal route vie Ramelton, Milford, Carrigart, Dunfanaghy and Falcarragh

As a direct route would prove less costly and the

Londonderry and Lough Swilly Railway Company were prepared to operate the route, this was given approval, but the exact route would need to be defined.

A great driver behind this decision was the need to bring greater prosperity to the Northwest.

A Government study of the area reported that in the neglected Northwest:

"There are two classes, namely the poor and the destitute. There are hardly any resident gentry; there are a few traders and officials; but nearly all the inhabitants are either poor or on the verge of poverty. The people are very helpful to one another, the poor mainly support the destitute".(1)

One of the measures instigated by the government was an attempt to open up the indigenous fishing industry to the markets of Derry, Belfast and Dublin.

As part of this strategy Burtonport harbour was extended and up graded, all they needed now was a rail link.

The Railways (Ireland) Act 1896 was a positive step forward as it provided funding for any company wishing to build a route.

The decision was taken to build a line from Letterkenny to Burtonport operated by 'The Swilly'.

This was given Privy Council approval on 10th February 1898.

Gweedore station opened on 9th March 1903, when the Londonderry and Lough Swilly Railway opened their Letterkenny and Burtonport Extension Railway, from Letterkenny to Burtonport.

It brought tourism on a greater scale to the Northwest with many taking holidays in the Gweedore area and enjoying the relative luxury of the Gweedore Railway Hotel. Now the An Chúirt, Gweedore Court Hotel & Earagail Health Club. This was first built in the 1830s by Lord George Hill, who was a landowner in the area.

However, concern was raised by the Board of works that 'The Swilly' was neglecting its stations and an inspection tour was undertaken in in May 1917, by Joseph Tatlow from the Midland Great Westerns headquarters in Dublin.

On May the 7th, Tatlow delivered this damming indictment of the state of Gweedore Railway station:

"This station, being in the centre of an important tourist district and having adjacent a well-known hotel, frequented by a good class of tourists, would by any self-respecting railway company be kept in a clean and tidy and as far as possible attractive condition. I am sorry to say that the reverse is the case: it is dirty, slovenly, untidy and very deficient of paint".(2)

Tatlow was not holding back, and he went on to report:

"The ladies' waiting room is a disgrace. It has a concrete floor which looks rude and uncouth. Gweedore is a well enough constructed station and with ordinary care and attention could be kept quite attractive looking. The palings of the station are in bad order. The stationmaster's office is on a lower level than the platform and his access to the latter is roundabout and awkward. The construction of a few steps to the platform would save him time and labour and be a great convince. The signal frame is on the platform and uncovered and frequently unworkable from frost and snow. It should be covered for protection and locked against interference when not in use".(3)

The Tatlow report did not just deal with Gweedore, the entire Swilly operated line was dealt a devastating blow with issues raised with stations, rolling stock and employees.

No railway company in Ireland had ever received such a damming report and the chairman of the Swilly resigned with promises to rectify the issues Tatlow had outlined. The Gweedore station was refurbished as part of the response.

The First World War was also having an impact on

the Swilly railway. One major issue was the reduction in the fishing stocks landed as men went to war and boats feared the U boats hunting the North Atlantic. Tourism also fell as the horrors of the Great War took hold.

In 1917 the entire Irish network was placed in the hands of a government committee.

The Donegal railway line would also witness civil unrest during the war years.

The first major event was on the 4th of January 1918 when two Nationalist Volunteers who had deserted from the British Army, James Duffy of Meenbanad, who had served in the Royal Dublin Fusiliers and James Ward of Cloughlass, who had served in the Royal Inniskilling Fusiliers, were arrested and held awaiting transfer to Derry.

A 4-man armed escort arrived in Burtonport, ready to take the men for trial in Derry. They spent the day in a local hostelry and were drunk when the train departed. It was soon stopped by a rescue party, supported by a large crowd of locals, who quickly disarmed the drunken escort and freed the prisoners.

This act is recognised as one of the first actions of the war of Independence that would soon set Ireland alight.

On May Day 1918 employees at Gweedore station joined with their colleagues in the Swilly and stopped work as part of the national protest against conscription.

During the War of Independence, IRA activity in

Donegal was stepped up and attacks against the railway network in Donegal increased. This was to isolate the Crown forces and to deny them supplies of food and ammunition. It was also to ensure captured volunteers were rescued as soon as possible.

From July 1920, Gweedore station staff, in common with their colleagues in 'The Swilly' refused to have anything to do with military transports or even civilian trains with Crown forces on-board! This was to be called the 'Munition's strike'.

The Burtonport line, including Gweedore was effectively shut down as train crew's feared Volunteer retaliation if they kept working.

On April 25th 1921, Gweedore station was entered by the IRA and goods from Belfast were destroyed. The telegraph lines at Crolly and Falcarragh were also cut.

On the 13th of July 1921, the IRA GHQ in Dublin issued orders for all closed railways including the Swilly to reopen for traffic. When the truce was signed train, services resumed to Letterkenny but Gweedore station and the Burtonport line did not reopen until 25th July.

The civil war saw further unrest on the Donegal railway.

The railways were now under attack and on March 31st, 1922, the Derry to Burtonport train was attacked at Newtoncunningham and copies of the Derry journal burnt. The paper sent more copies only for these to be intercepted and burnt.

The campaign was aimed at food merchandise and newspapers from the north that were all destroyed when found on trains. Such was the intensity of the disruptions that on April 29th 1922, the Swilly announced that they could no longer guarantee a reliable service and they refused to accept any further responsibility for any losses from disturbances.

In early 1923 locals in Gweedore and the Rosses met in Dungloe where inhabitants and merchants voiced their lack of confidence in the Londonderry and Lough Swilly Company and called on the fledgling Irish Government to transfer the Letterkenny to Burtonport line to the Strabane and Letterkenny Railway Company.

This request was refused, and things only got worse for the Swilly when border customs posts where introduced on the line in April 1923.

## OWENCARROW VIADUCT DISASTER

Tragedy was to strike the line on the night of 30th January 1925 at around 8pm at the Owencarrow Viaduct, outside Kilmacrennan.

On that evening, an engine pulling two carriages, one wagon, and a combined van, was travelling on the

Londonderry and Lough Swilly Railway Burtonport Extension.

The 14 passengers had been enjoying the journey, having left Kilmacrennan Station at 7:52pm, running only five minutes late.

It was a wild and stormy night and at around 8pm the train approached the Owencarrow Viaduct which was considered by the drivers as dangerous in bad weather. However, the driver later reported that he did not see anything unusual.

Travelling at 10 miles an hour the train entered the viaduct, which was nearly 440 yards in length. When the train was a little more than 60 yards onto the viaduct, there was a great gust of wind, which lifted the carriage next to the engine off the rails.

The driver applied the vacuum brake and stopped the train. When the train came to a halt, the back carriage, which had been lifted off, had carried the wagons halfway over the wall of the bridge. The other carriage was lying over the embankment, its roof torn off throwing four passengers to their deaths:

Mr. Philip Boyle, Leabgarrow, Arranmore

Mrs. Sarah Boyle, Leabgarrow, Arranmore (wife of Philip)

Neil Duggan, Meenabunone and Mrs. Una Mulligan, Falcarragh.

Five others were seriously injured:

Mrs. Brennan, Dungloe – severe injuries to her head

Mrs. McFadden, sister-in-law of Mrs. Brennan – shock

Mrs. Bella McFadden, Gweedore – shock

Edward McFadden, Magheraroarty–shock and wounded hand

Denis McFadden, Cashel, Creeslough – severe concussion

One passenger a Miss Campbell had a lucky escape.

She was flung from the upturned carriage, landing on soft and boggy soil, sinking knee-deep into it.

The subsequent inquest cleared the Driver and blamed the accident on the decaying state of the line, it was obvious 'The Swilly' had not learned the lessons of the Tatlow report.

You can see the remains of the Viaduct If you take the N56 from Creeslough heading to Letterkenny,

## THE END OF THE LINE

The 'Emergency' – as World War II was called in Ireland – proved a great strain on the Donegal railway network.

In May 1940 'The Swilly' announced that from the 3Rd of June 1940 as a result of a government statutory order, the Letterkenny to Burtonport line was to be closed and the lines dug up.

The reasons given for the closure were a decline in traffic and the prohibitive costs of the repairs needed on the network.

While the odd goods train still travelled to Burton-port, the end was coming and in August 1940 the firm of George Cohen and company were employed to start digging up the railway tracks from the Burtonport end.

Dismayed and angry at the removal of their rail network, the people of Northwest Donegal protested at the closure. On the 18th of November 1940, 100 men gathered at Crolly to block the demolition work of the Cohen Company.

The Guards and a local TD calmed the crowd by promising that the government would review the decision to close the line and that demolition would be temporarily halted.

This was to prove only a short reprieve, because on the 29th of November, the decision to close the line was upheld.

However, by now with oil and petrol rationing in full flow, travel by road was no alternative to rail and 'The Swilly' decided to halt the demolition of the remainder of the line and permission was sought to reopen the Letterkenny to Gweedore line.

On the 14th of January 1941 a goods train left Letterkenny for Gweedore returning with a consignment of Herring for the Belfast market. This proved that the line whilst in disrepair was passable. A decision was taken that a dilapidated line was better than no line at all.

Services began again on the 3rd of February 1941 when the Letterkenny to Gweedore line reopened for freight traffic.

From March 1943 passengers were also allowed to officially travel the route. Many had done so unofficially from 1941 onwards!

By the end of the war years, the company was carrying nearly 500,000 passengers per annum on its rail services from Derry to Buncranna and Gweedore.

With the ending of hostilities and the restoration of petrol and oil supplies, the company re-embarked on its policy of replacing rail services by road transport as vehicles became available and more economically viable!

As the 'Emergency' ended, the line from Letterkenny to Gweedore was in a dangerous state of disrepair. The daily goods service between Letterkenny and Gweedore was withdrawn in January 1947. However, a few special trains operated until June of that year when the line finally closed.

Lifting of the line took place in 1949.

The rest of 'The Swilly' line would limp on for just a few more years.

The last train to run on 'The Swilly' line was the 2.15pm from Letterkenny to Derry on 8th August 1953.

It included 14 wagons of cattle and arrived 50 minutes late.

Bob Turner was the driver with Paddy Clifford as fireman. The Derry Journal reported at the time

"The guard, Mr. Daniel McFeeley, or anyone else, did not call out 'Next Stop Derry'. Everyone knew that the next stop would be the last stop - the last ever."(4)

Lifting of the lines commenced almost immediately and was completed in early 1954.

Such was the attachment to the Donegal railways that after the line from Donegal Town to Ballyshannon closed down in 1959, two of the railway workers continued to operate a freight service between the two towns for a month before the bosses in Dublin realised what was happening.

In modern day Ireland intercity rail passenger services operate between Dublin and Belfast, Sligo, Ballina, Westport, Galway, Limerick, Ennis, Tralee, Cork, Waterford and Rosslare.

Europort and Iarnród Éireann jointly operates the Dublin to Belfast Enterprise service with Northern Ireland Railways.

Regional services include the new Limerick to Galway line, Cork commuter network including the new Cork-Middletown line, Limerick Junction to Waterford, and Limerick to Ballybrophy (via Nenagh) services.

In addition to the DART service, which operates between Greystones and Howth/Malahide.

They also run the commuter service in the Dublin area between Gorey, Drogheda, the new M3 Parkway line and Maynooth, as well as the commuter service to Kildare.

However, no trains operate in one of Ireland's largest counties the forgotten Donegal and Gweedore station is no more.

*Sources:*

1. *Hansard*
2. *Fifty Years of Railway Life in England, Scotland and Ireland, Joseph Tatlow*
3. *Fifty Years of Railway Life in England, Scotland and Ireland, Joseph Tatlow*
4. *Derry Journal, August 1954*

# CHAPTER 15
# LORD GEORGE HILL, THE MODERNISING LANDLORD

Lord George Augusta Hill the 3rd was an Irish military officer, politician, landlord and author.

He would go on to marry not one but two nieces of Jane Austen and become somewhat of a poster boy for Victorian Anglo-Irish landlordism in Ireland following the publication of his book 'Facts from Gweedore' in 1845. This was his account of the conditions of his tenants in Gweedore and the defence of the agricultural and structural reforms that he implemented in his estates from 1838 onwards.

While many other Landlords strived to copy Hills draconian reforms, the House of Commons select committee on Irish Poverty was less enthusiastic and even went as far as to investigate his methods.

Lord George Hill was a flamboyant and complex character, and this is his story.

George Hill was born on the 9th of December 1801, the 7th and last child of Arthur Hill the 2nd Marquis of Downshire and Mary Baroness Sandys.

Arthur Hill while Governor of Down and a member of the Privy Council of Ireland vigorously opposed the union of the UK and Irish parliaments. His reward was to be removed as Governor and stripped of his place on the Privy Council. Humiliated he committed suicide in September 1801 just three months before the birth of his Son. George was always a favourite of his mother who had lost her husband just months before his birth. With no prospect of inheriting his late father's titles, his options of advancement lay in either a good marriage or a military career.

Aged just 16, he joined the Army as a Cornet in the Royal Horse Guards. This was the third and lowest grade of commissioned officer in a British cavalry troop, after captain and lieutenant. It is equivalent to a modern day second lieutenant.

He was promoted to lieutenant in 1820. Five years later he was transferred to the Royal Irish Dragoons as Captain. He served throughout the north of Ireland on what were termed 'peace keeping' duties.

In the general election of 1826, he was proposed to stand for the town of Carrickfergus where his brother owned some land. He would later withdraw his nomination claiming he did not know he had been put forward.

In April 1830 at the relatively young age of 29, he was made 'Aide de camp' to Sir John Byng, the commander in chief of the crown forces in Ireland, with the rank of Major. In June of that year, he joined what was coined the half pay list. This was the pay or allowance an officer received when in retirement or not in actual service.(1)

He did so out of family duty, he was required by his brother the 3rd Marquis of Downshire to stand in the election which was triggered by the death of King George IV and produced the first parliament of the reign of his successor, William IV.

The election was fought in the aftermath of the 'Swing Riots', which were a widespread uprising in 1830 by agricultural workers in southern and eastern England, in protest of agricultural mechanisation and other harsh working conditions, it saw electoral reform become the major issue of the election.

George was once again proposed for the seat of Carrickfergus and decided to stand this time. After a hard fought and dirty battle, he was duly elected as a supporter of the Duke of Wellingtons faction in the new parliament of September 1830.

Despite being recognised as a supporter of Welling-ton, Hill was ever his own man and he failed to attend the vote of confidence in Wellington's administration on the 15th of November 1830, his absence helped bring the Dukes premiership to an end.

He then became an enthusiastic supporter with his brothers of the new government of Earl Grey who led the Whig faction who would go onto pass the great reform Act of 1832. This introduced major changes to the voting system of England and Wales.

Now this enthusiasm didn't stretch to speaking in the House of Commons, as George never uttered one speech in his parliamentary career, which came to an end in 1832, when he resigned claiming ill health.(2)

He returned to Ireland to help his brother Lord Marcus Hill be elected the MP for Newry.(3)

His health seemingly restored in 1833, George Hill was soon appointed the comptroller in the household of the Lord Lieutenant of Ireland.

The following year on the 21st of October 1834, Lord George Hill married Cassandra Jane Night the daughter of Edward Austen Knight, the brother of the novelist Jane Austen. They would go on to have four children.

Norah Mary Elizabeth Hill (12 December 1835 – 24 April 1920)

Captain Arthur Blundell George Sandys Hill (13 May 1837 – 16 June 1923)

Augustus Charles Edward Hill (9 March 1839 – 9 December 1908)

Cassandra Jane Louisa Hill (12 March 1842 – 16 August 1901)

In March 1838 he sold his commission in the 47th regiment of foot and using funds provided by his late mother's will and other family members, he purchased land in Gweedore county Donegal. He would go on to expand his holdings to 23,000 acres including a number of offshore islands, the largest of which was Gola island.

Gweedore in 1838 was part of the parish of Tullaghbegley. Its landscape was mountainous lakes and bogs with patches of arable land which swept down to the wild Atlantic Ocean.

The population was about 3,000 souls, 700 of whom paid rent and who almost universally spoke the Irish language with few if any with much English. They were Roman Catholic with a strong faith and education was rare and offered to very few by a local school master.

Grazing of cattle, rearing of small livestock, growing potatoes on patches of land and seasonal fishing were the main ways of subsidence living, as luxuries were few and far between.

The area lacked no real infrastructure with roads in a deplorable state. In 1837 the Lord Lieutenant of Ireland on his tour of Ireland was appalled by the state of the roads and was barely able to travel through Gweedore.

During his journey he was petitioned by the local

School master Peter McKye who pleaded for assistance saying that:

"That the parishioners of this parish of Tullaghobegly, in the Barony of Kilmacrennan, are in the most, needy, hungry, and naked condition of any people that ever came within the precincts of my knowledge, although I have travelled a part of nine counties in Ireland, also a part of England and Scotland, together with a part of British America. I have likewise perambulated 2,253 miles through some of the United States, and never witnessed the tenth part of such hunger, hardships, and nakedness".(4)

It was into this seemingly backward and impoverished parish that Lord George Hill came as a landlord and unlike others before him he was determined to stay and change Gweedore forever. Hill also had an advantage that many other Anglo-Irish landlords did not have. He knew and spoke Gaelic, the main language of the people of Gweedore.

His first impressions of Gweedore were not favorable. In his book Facts on Gweedore written in 1845 he described Gweedore as:

"Ruled by a few bullies, and lawless distillers, who acknowledged neither landlord or agent; and the absence of anything like roads effectively kept civilization from the district and prevented people bringing more land into cultivation."(5)

Again, in 'Facts from Gweedore', he described condition of the people of Gweedore when he arrived as:

"More deplorable than can well be conceived; famine was periodical and fever its attendant; wretchedness pervaded the district."(6)

His first task was to change the inhabitant's perception of paying rent, which was reluctant and sporadic at best. In 1834 it was recorded that two revenue police parties" were "beaten and disarmed" and "fifty constabulary were repulsed and forced to give up collecting the tithe.(7) He believed that the best way to modernise Gweedore, would be to end the Rundale system and ensure the payment of rents.

The Rundale system of land holding was prevalent in the western part of Ireland before the famine. In this system, the land was leased to one or two tenants, who then divvied it up amongst 20-30 others (in many cases the whole town).

The land was held in joint tenancy (a partnership of tenants).

Under the Rundale system the land was divided into

several areas based on varying land quality. An "infield area" that was composed of land to grow crops and an "outfield" area further out that was used for grazing usually radiated out from the homes.(8)

England had this sort of "infield/outfield" system in place in which the village (clachan as it was referred to in Ireland) was surrounded by the highest quality land (infield), more distantly bordered by the more inferior grazing area.

The land was distributed amongst the tenants based on the amount of rent contributed. The different pieces of land within the rundale were shuffled periodically to promote a fair distribution of poor, middle of the road and quality land.

This was an ancient form of land division that, despite its faults, allowed everyone access to the best land, water and common grazing. It also allowed subdivision of lots to accommodate the need for sons to have their own farms. One disadvantage of the Rundale system was that holdings were often scattered small plots, spread over a wide area and, because of this, holdings were not fenced, creating additional problems with wandering stock.

Houses were clustered into "clachans," a group of houses of the families who tenanted the surrounding Rundale. The clachans were often just one room, with the family living at one end and the animals living at the other. Grazing of animals was also done on a rotational basis and families often moved with their animals between mountain pasture, lowland, and the islands.

Apart from the grazing of sheep and cows the land was cultivated for potatoes (to eat) and oats (to pay the rent).

Despite being by the sea the people of Gweedore did extraordinarily little fishing.

A government report from 1837 described that:

"On the mainland in the Gweedore District there are not now any fishermen. The Islanders on the Coast contrive to exist, and to increase and multiply beyond measure, on the produce of the soil (potatoes), and to pay their rent and taxes; but in seasons of dearth, which occur on and average of every fourth year, they are as destitute as the poor on the mainland. Famines have occurred on the islands only when experienced on the coast."(9)

Hill believed that the small-scale fishing was down to competition from boats from other areas and more importantly the that the price of salt, needed for the preservation of fish, was also prohibitive, as it had to be brought long distances to Gweedore.

Being by the sea did have some advantages as the

fields were improved by the addition of sand and seaweed, to fertilize and break up the peaty soil.

Lord George Hill believed the Rundale system was a barrier to his plans to introduce more modern and profitable farming methods and his desire to bring sheep into Gweedore. He would later describe the system in 'Facts from Gweedore' as: "The cause of "fights, trespasses, confusion, disputes and assaults."(10)

Lord Hill also began improving the transport infrastructure in Gweedore. The first road was built in 1834 by the Board of Works from Dunlewey to the Gweedore River. A series of roads were then built throughout the Gweedore estate.

At Bunbeg, Hill built a harbor, a grain store and created a general store which sold a wide variety of merchandise. He even set up a bakery importing a Scottish baker by the name of Mason.

The creation of the grain store was no philanthropic exercise, it had a twofold objective. The first was to control the supply and price of grain and ensure that his tenants would not only grow the crop but once they sold it, they would have capital to then pay his rents.

Secondly by controlling the grain supply he hoped to discourage the distillation of grain alcohol and end what he perceived to be a scourge of drunkenness throughout his estate. In later years Hill would admit he was not successful in this endeavor!

Hill was also ruthless in ensuring his new enterprises had no competition. He even went as far as to evict one of his tenants a Margaret Sweeney who set up a bakery without his permission.

Lord Hill's long-term plan was to introduce large scale sheep farming in Gweedore and in preparation for this he contracted the London firm of Allen and Solly who set up an agency in Bunbeg.

They would supply wool (which would eventually come from Hills's sheep) and purchase knitted products. The local population had always made their own clothing and knitted garments from the small-scale sheep farming in the area. This initiative was extremely popular and was estimated to inject £500 per annum into the local economy.

In a bid to encourage tourism in the area, Lord George Hill constructed a hotel, which was designed to emulate the highland lodges of Scotland, designed for visitors to enjoy fishing, and hunting in the local area.

He also created what was known as a model farm beside the hotel to showcase the modern techniques he wished his tenants to adopt.

In his push to end the Rundale system, Hill began an exercise to survey his estate between 1841 and 1843. He used the results to allocate new holdings to each tenant.

Hill did not get everything his own way. His original

plan was to square each plot, but this faced fierce opposition and a compromise was reached.

It was agreed that each tenant's new holdings would be aggregated into strips rather than squares. Each strip included both infield and outfield land and access to water. The advantages they received under the old Rundale system.

However, this new allocation meant that the clachan style of housing (a cluster of small single-storey cottages of farmers) was to end and new houses were to be built on each new holding, at the tenant's expense.

Hill even went so far as to outlaw the building of any new houses and the further subdivision of land or the sale of tenants' rights.

The prohibition on any further land subdivision was a particularly draconian act as it meant that no family could provide land for their sons or daughters. This meant that emigration was usually the only option for them.

In another attempt to improve the land on his estate, Hill offered prizes to his tenants for best kept cottage, best vegetables and healthiest livestock. It was initially rebuffed by his tenants but over time they began to participate enthusiastically.

Lord Hill did however, bar anyone from entering who was found to be producing poteen, who had been convicted of breach of the peace or who was behind with their rent.

In March of 1842 tragedy struck when Hills's wife Cassandra Jane died two days after the birth of their 4th child, Cassandra Jane Louisa.

Cassandra's sister Louisa Knight who was Jane Austin's God daughter moved to Ireland to look after Hill's children.

Women often died in childbirth, and their unmarried sisters, who had few other options to support themselves besides marriage, would step in to care for the family. For convenience, and sometimes developing love, remarriage seemed like the thing to do.

George and Louisa would eventually marry on the 11th of May 1847.

The marriage was controversial and even prompted an investigation in the UK parliament looking at the legality of a marriage between a widower and his deceased wife's sister. The issue was:

"whether a man's wife's sister was, in law, the equivalent of his blood sister and therefore never to be his wife, or his metaphorical sister only and therefore an 'indifferent person' whom he could marry".(11)

The marriage was not contested, and they would go on to have a happy marriage and one son George.

In 1845 as was common for many Landlords, Lord George Hill was appointed the High Sheriff of Donegal which was the British Crown's judicial representative in County Donegal from the late 16th century until 1922, when the office was abolished in the new Irish Free State and replaced by the office of Donegal County Sheriff. The High Sheriff had judicial, electoral, ceremonial and administrative functions and executed High Court Writs. Also, in 1845, as Famine began to stalk the Irish landscape Lord George Hill published his book 'Facts From Gweedore'. It would eventually run to five editions and played a major role in the often-bitter public debates about the effects of Irish landlordism in post-famine Ireland.

Professor Evans of the Institute of Irish Studies of Queens University, Belfast describes the booklet as: "The most detailed account we have of the rural world of the Gael, of its cultural and physical attributes in the days before the great famine."(12)

And in Hill himself he saw, "an outstanding and in many ways an exceptional figure among Irish landlords of the nineteenth century."(13)

Father James McFadden the parish priest of nearby Falcarragh and a land league campaigner who would become the parish priest of Gweedore in 1875, had a rather more cynical view of the book. He called it:

"This is a summary of the alleged facts from Gweedore, which might, perhaps, with more regard to truth and accuracy be called "Fictions from Gweedore", conceived, arranged, and printed by the Lord of the Soil himself, to dispose public opinion, to receive with equanimity the shock and outrage imparted to it by the cruel, not to say, unjust action of doubling the rents, appropriating immemorial rights, and otherwise oppressing an already rack rented and harassed tenantry."(14)

Perhaps Father McFadden who was a constant thorn in Hills side in his later life had an ulterior motive to denigrate Facts from Gweedore. As a member of the Land League and a campaigner for tenants' rights and no friend of landlords, McFadden was determined to highlight the negative impact of Hill, whom McFadden believed was guilty of: "Tyranny and oppression against his tenants"... and "spoliation and appropriation" of their lands."(15)

The fighting priests own view of Gweedore before the advent of Hill's arrival was much more positive than other commentators. He wrote:

"Before the advent of Lord George Hill, Gweedore had no history, -at least no history recorded in the suffering and sorrows of an oppressed and landlord ridden people. In this regard there was a profound peace. There was amongst its inhabitants' comfort, if not actual comfort, at least equal comfort with their neighbors and the rest of Ireland, and comfort much above their present condition, as testified by the bailiff, who is not accused of leanings to the popular side. Before the advent of Lord George Hill there were no appeals year after year. There were no wails of distress and starvation ascending from the valleys of Gweedore season after season. But after his arrival there has been going on a bitter war from that day to this."(16)

My own view is that readers should be more sceptical and understand why 'Facts for Gweedore' was written, before looking at its historical accuracy.

It was Lord George Hills intention to achieve two objectives with the publication of his book. The first was purely financial to encourage tourism and visitors to his newly build hotel.

The second was more personal, to paint Hill in a positive light. He wanted to show that the improvements he had made in farming methods, manufacturing and infrastructure had improved the lives of his tenants. He wished to be recognised as a benevolent landlord in an era of land wars, famine and the turmoil of eviction.

No matter how well Lord Hill wished to portray his agricultural changes, the majority of his tenants were subsistence farmer's dependant on grain and livestock to pay their rent and potatoes to live. They were one bad harvest away from famine.

Potato blight was not new to Ireland and partial crop failures were recorded in 1831, 1837, 1854 and 1856. A complete failure of the potato crop in 1845 heralded 'An Gorta Mór' the great Irish famine of 1845 to 1849. The great hunger was a period of mass starvation, disease but above all state negligence. The worst year of the famine was 1847 known as 'Black 47'.

It is estimated that at least one million people died from starvation and its attendant diseases, whilst a further one million emigrated during the famine years. The population of Ireland dropped from over eight million in 1845 to about six million in 1850. Gweedore did not escape the horrors of Black 47.

Barry D Hewitson, writing, from Gweedore to the Belfast Ladies Association for the Relief of Destitution in 1847 said:

"I have just returned after a day of painful exertion...in one house I found a family of fourteen the eldest fourteen years of age, the youngest nine weeks - the mother unable to leave her bed since its birth. They had not a morsel of food in the house... I went to another house to inquire about a young woman who had been employed on the public works and had gone away ill during the severe snowstorm. On reaching home she complained of great coldness; her mother and father made her go to bed (the only one in the house); she fell into a sleep from which she never woke. This day her poor mother died also, and there are two of the children who, I am sure, will not be alive by tomorrow, to such a state are they reduced from bad and insufficient food. Lord George Hill is doing all that a man can do. He is occupied from morning till night sparing himself neither trouble nor personal fatigue."(17)

Lord Hill's attitude to the famine was harsh and some would say even cruel but not uncommon among the Anglo-Irish aristocracy He wrote:

"The Irish people have profited much by the Famine, the lesson was severe; but so were they rooted in old prejudices and old ways, that no teacher could have induced them to make the changes which this Visitation of Divine Providence has brought about, both in their habits of life and in their mode of agriculture."(18)

Despite this, it must be said that Lord Hill unlike many of his contemporary's did at least try to help his tenants. He appealed for funds to alleviate the hardship to organizations such as the Society of Friends (the

Quakers), the Irish Peasantry Improvement Society of London and the Baptist Society for funds.

One government tactic during the famine, which led to so much hardship and death was to protect the price of grain and only sell at the prevailing market prices. Lord George Hill again unlike so many landlords decided to sell grain to his tenants at a loss. The Corn Mill in Bunbeg proved a fortuitous enterprise and ground 688 tons of Indian corn to mitigate the hardship of the famine.

However, some were not impressed, and later Father McFadden was again harsh in his criticism:

"He [Hill] got over £700 from Government for grinding Indian corn in 1847!! The meagre outdoor relief he gave to some tenants of a stone of meal in the week or fort-night, was to keep them out of the workhouse."(19)

During the famine Ireland's population fell by between 20% and 25%, however perhaps due to the fruits of the wild Atlantic, especially edible seaweed and the actions of Lord George Hill the population of Gwee-dore, whilst suffering hardship actually rose.

This is backed up by the census of 1851, which showed that compared to ten years earlier the popula-tion of Gweedore increased slightly despite the ravages of the famine. Of course, people did die but in the parish of Tullaghbegley (of which Gweedore is the western section) there was a decrease in population of less than 1% from 1841 to 1851.(20)

Furthermore, in eighteen of the most populous of Lord George Hill's townlands there was an 8% increase in population over the same period, which Hill claimed was proof that his drive for modernity helped negate the worst of the famine.(21)

In February 1858 Hills tenure in Gweedore was attacked in the press where an appeal by ten catholic priests including Daniel McGee, P.P. Gweedore and James McFadden C.C. Cloughaneely was published in the press:

"In the wilds of Donegal, down in the bogs and glens of Gweedore and Cloughaneely, thousands and thousands of human beings, made after the image and likeness of God, are perishing, or next to perishing, amid squalidness and misery, for want of food and clothing, far away from aid and pity. On behalf of these famishing victims of oppression and persecution, we appeal for substantial assistance to enable us to relieve their wretchedness and rescue them from death and starvation.

There are at the moment 800 families subsisting on seaweed, crabs, cockles, or any other edible matter they can pick up along the seashore or scrape off the rocks.

There are about 600 adults of both sexes, who through sheer poverty are now going barefoot, amid the inclemency of the season, on this bleak northern coast. There are about 700 families that have neither bed nor bedclothes... Thousands of the male population have only one cotton shirt, while thousands have not even one. There are about 600 families who have neither cow, sheep, nor goat and who hardly know the taste of milk or butter. This fine old Celtic race is about being crushed to make room for Scotch and English sheep."(22)

A relief committee was established, and this stark imagery prompted a parliamentary select committee to be established in June 1858 to investigate the claims of extreme poverty in Gweedore.

The committee heard evidence from a wide variety of witnesses. Some claimed destitution and poverty were rife and others claimed Lord Hill tenure was a success.

On one side were the Landlord Lord Hill and members of the local gentry including visitors to Hill's hotel that claimed that no such poverty existed.

On the other, were the clergy and tenants who maintained that destitution was rife and poverty endemic.

One witness a reporter from the Dublin Evening post, James Williams, testified that what he saw in Gweedore was: "The most deplorably degraded state of destitution that I ever saw."(23) He went on to say that it was his impression that: "It was the determination of Lord George Hill to exterminate the entire race."(24)

A more balanced view came from local priest Fr Doherty who gave Lord George Hill credit for building roads, a shop, a post office, and a quay at Bunbeg. He also went as far to say Hill had saved many from dying during the famine. His grievance was that poverty was being created by the removal of the mountain grazing, which was an actual harm to his people's livelihoods.

This was because on Lord George Hill's land, approximately 23,000 acres, about 12,000 was left to the tenants and the rest was leased to Scotsmen, for the grazing of sheep.

He also wished to introduce deer for his hotel guests to hunt.

One thing all witnesses agreed on was that the people of Gweedore out of necessity had to eat seaweed. However, again this was from two different perspectives. Those that claimed there was no destitution claimed that it was a nutritional resource greatly benefiting the population. Others countered this by saying with no alternative this was a clear sign of destitution.

No one denied either that the rents had gone up, but Hill claimed that the total rateable value of his townlands had been increased by bringing more land into production, while, for others, it was clearly exploitation by Lord Hill.

Lord George Hill gave his evidence to the committee on the 23rd and 24th of June.

It came as no surprise that the select committee found in the Landlord's favour and declared that there was no evidence of destitution, saying:

"... it appears to Your [Queen Victoria's] committee that destitution, such as complained of in the Appeal of 8 January 1858, did not and does not exist..." The statements of the appeal "are not borne out by the evidence taken before them; and Your committee have come to the conclusion that those representations are calculated to convey to the public a false and erroneous impression of the state of the people in this district As to the claim that the Landlords took away the mountain grazing, a claim crucial to the priests case, the Committee decided this to be "totally devoid of foundation."(25)

This not unexpected decision did not deter the relief committee who went on to raise £2,196 5s 7d. Up to the time of the Select Committee hearing they had given out £1,600 worth of clothing, seed and money.

The activity of the parish priests of both Gweedore and Falcarragh earned the loyalty of the people and were therefore seen to be a nuisance by the authorities.

Constable William Young of the Gweedore Constabulary accused the Catholic Priests of interfering in the land-lord's business.

Lord Hill continued with his drive to modernise Gweedore but was increasingly worn down by the rising opposition to his plans. With the arrival of Father McFadden in Gweedore in late 1875, Hills troubles increased, it was the bailiff's opinion that the people of Gweedore were under the "complete authority" of Fr McFadden.

In ill health Hill retreated increasingly to his home Ballyare House in Ramelton, where he died on the 6th of April 1879 (aged 77). He was buried at Conwal Parish Church in Letterkenny, alongside Cassandra Jane Knight the first Austen to whom he was married.

So ended the life of the man who was elected to parliament but never spoke, an MP who helped bring down Wellingtons Government, the landlord who could speak Irish and the man who married not one but two nieces of Jane Austen.

A memorial plague was erected on the outside wall of the Church of Ireland church in Bunbeg which said:

"Sacred to the memory of Lord George Hill. A self-denying Christian, he devoted his life and fortune to civilize Gweedore and raise its people to a higher social and moral level."

Some residents of Gweedore disagreed and due to constant vandalism, the plague is now situated on a wall behind the altar.

His son captain Arthur Hill inherited the Gweedore estate and would now begin a battle of wills with Father McFadden a land league activist and no friend of landlordism who would go onto be called the fighting priest of Gweedore.

*Sources:*

1. *Belfast Newsletter, April 16, 1830*
2. *History of Parliament*
3. *Newry Commercial Telegraph, January 4, 1833*
4. *Memorial of Paddy McKye, Gweedore, 1837 (donegalgenealogy.com)*
5. *Facts from Gweedore, Lord George Hill, 1845*
6. *Facts from Gweedore, Lord George Hill, 1845*
7. *Facts from Gweedore, Lord George Hill, 1845*
8. *Irish Geography website*
9. *Report of the Commissioners of Inquiry into the State of the Irish Fisheries, House of Commons Sessional Papers, Vol XXII, 1837*
10. *Facts from Gweedore, Lord George Hill, 1845*
11. *'On the Deceased Wife's Sister Controversy, 1835-1907', Anne D. Wallace*

12. *His life and fortune to civilise Gweedore: RTE documentary, May 4, 1975*

13. *His life and fortune to civilise Gweedore: RTE documentary, May 4, 1975*

14. *JJ McFadden: The past and present 15 JJ McFadden: The past and present 16 JJ McFadden: The past and present*

15. *The Famine in Ulster: The Regional Impact, Ulster Historical Foundation, Belfast, 1997*

16. *Introductory chapter to the third edition of 'Facts from Gweedore', Richard Hill, 1853*

17. *JJ McFadden: The past and present*

18. *British House of Commons Sessional Papers, 1852-53, vol XCII, p. 132*

19. *British House of Commons Sessional Papers, 1852-53, vol XCII, p. 132*

20. *Freeman's Journal, February 12, 1858*

21. *Parliamentary Report 1858 questions 1234-1251*

22. *Parliamentary Report 1858 questions 1234-1251*

23. *Parliamentary Report 1858 Gweedore p91*

# CHAPTER 16

# THE GREAT FLOOD IN GWEEDORE—DEATH IN ST MARY'S

On the 15th of August 1880 tragedy struck the parish of Gweedore, while parish priest Father James McFadden said Mass in a packed St Mary's Chapel in Derrybeg. This is known in Gweedore as the great flood, while the Irish Times would describe the event as the Gweedore catastrophe.

The 15th of August was the feast of the Assumption of Mary, and the local church of St Mary's in Gweedore was full with many parishioners standing around the chapel.

On that fateful day, a freak storm broke out and a deluge was thrown from the heavens as thunder rang out. The church was built in a ravine where mass had been said in secret during the penal laws which outlawed the Catholic rites, and a mountain stream ran under the floor of the church.

Soon that stream was overflowing and within minutes of the storm, the water rose up through the floor and the masonry gave way to a deadly torrent that engulfed the worshipers.

The doors became jarred by the rising tide and people began scrambling out of the windows. Water levels inside the church rose to an estimated 12 feet in a matter of minutes

Father McFadden the parish priest now aware that fatalities had taken place began to give general absolution to the congregation and then made his own escape jumping from the altar smashing a window and making to safety. Sadly five parishioners died and over 100 were injured.

The youngest who died was 13-year-old altar server Séamus Ó Fearraigh of Stranacorkra, Derrybeg.

The others who were drowned were Grace McGarvey, Carrick, Derrybeg, Conal Boyle, Inishmaan Island, and Enrí Ó Gallchobhair and Neil Doherty, both of Magheraclogher, Bunbeg.

To fully understand the tragedy, it is necessary to look at the history of Ireland and Gweedore to see why the Chapel of St Marys was built where it was in a remote ravine over a river and susceptible to flooding.

This unsuitable location ensured that the deluge which engulfed the unfortunate parishioners whilst a freak event of nature created more damage than was necessary to both parishioners and the building.

This was because of two things, firstly the restrictive penal laws imposed on Irish Catholics and secondly the refusal of successive protestant landowners in Gweedore to allow a catholic church to be built on suitable land.

## THE PENAL LAWS IN IRELAND

The penal laws were a series of statutes imposed by various English monarchs to coerce the native Irish who were predominantly Roman Catholic to convert to the protestant religion.

Various acts passed in the 16th and 17th centuries prescribed fines and imprisonment for participation in Catholic worship and severe penalties, including death, for Catholic priests who practiced their ministry.

After the surrender of Limerick in 1691 by the remnants of the forces of King James the 2nd the victorious King William assured religious freedom for his Irish subjects.

However, this assurance was of course made with strings attached. Every Roman Catholic was forced to take an oath of loyalty to King William and Queen Mary within a year.

William was initially comfortable granting freedom of worship to the Roman Catholic Irish, he had after all been supported in his quest for the crown and his campaign in Ireland by his ally Pope Alexander VIII who had given his blessing to his conflict against King James.

This all changed in 1693 when Alexander's successor Pope Innocent XII switched his support to the exiled King James. A furious William wary of a Roman Catholic uprising in Ireland became less tolerant of his Roman Catholic subjects many of whom were now less willing to swear allegiance.

William and Mary put forward a bill in the protestant controlled Irish Parliament in 1695 outlawing the catholic clergy. This was eventually passed into law in 1697.

The Irish parliament stuffed with protestant lords and landlords was now viciously anti Roman Catholic. Following the death of King William in 1702 they took greater steps towards restrictions against Catholics holding land, office or freely worshiping.

The Irish Parliament was actively encouraged by their English counterpart and Queen Anne ll the Protestant daughter of James ll and sister-in-law of William.

## THE PENAL LAWS IN IRELAND

The major Anti Roman Catholic laws in Ireland included: Exclusion of Catholics from holding public office such as a Judge, MP, solicitor, Jurist, barrister, civil servant, sheriff, or town councillor.

No Catholic could vote or be elected to office.

A ban was imposed upon Catholics from owning land. Catholics could not lease land for longer than thirty-one years and the rent was to equal two-thirds of the yearly value of the land.

Catholics were not allowed to hold arms nor be members of the armed forces nor own a horse worth more than £5.

If a Catholic landholder died, his estate could not be passed to the eldest son unless that son was a Protestant. Otherwise, it was to be shared by all the surviving sons.

A ban imposed upon intermarriage between Catholics and Protestants.

Catholic could not be an orphan's guardian.

Catholics were barred from living in many provincial towns.

Catholic clergy were to be registered and required to take an oath of loyalty, but friars, monks, hierarchy and Jesuits were to be exiled.

No cleric could wear distinguishing clothes.

Places of worship could not have a steeple nor display a cross.

Catholics and dissenters were required to pay tithes to the Anglican Church of Ireland which was the Established Church.

Catholics could not establish schools or send their children abroad for education.

Despite this raft of laws and state sponsored oppression most of the Irish population remained Roman Catholic and faithful to the celebration of Mass.

The Penal laws created two new traditions, the Mass Rock and Station Mass.

To avoid arrest Catholic priests and worshippers had to find hidden areas in the Irish countryside to celebrate Mass. 'Priest Hunters' were employed to seek out and arrest unregistered priests.

Many of these places of worship were marked with "Mass Rocks". The Mass Rock was oftentimes a rock taken from a church ruin and used as a place of worship for Roman Catholics.

Usually, the priest arrived in disguise and placed the sacred vessels on the rock while assigned locals kept a look-out from vantage points in the landscape from where they could see any approaching English militia. There are still many Mass rocks all over Ireland, the faithful still consider them to be sacred places.

In Irish, the name given to a 'Mass Rock' was Carraig an Aifrinn. Other names associated with sites where Mass was celebrated in Penal times include Clais an Aifrinn meaning 'Mass Ravine', Páirc an tSéipéil or 'Chapel field',

Faill an Aifrinn or 'Mass cliff ', Leaca na hAltorach

indicating a flat stone or rock altar, Cábán an Aifrinn or 'Mass Cabin', Cnocan na hAltorach meaning 'small hill of the altar' and Gleann an Aifrinn indicating a 'Mass Glen'. In many instances, the 'Mass Rock' was a stone taken from a ruined church and relocated to an isolated rural area, and a simple cross was carved on top.

Because the practice of the Roman Catholic Mass and other rites were illegal, the services were held at random times and places with the parishioners having to spread the word from neighbour to neighbour. By the late 17th century these rites of worship had been generally moved to thatched Mass houses, and the 'Mass Rock 'locations became used as places where the local faithful could make their devotions on the feast day of the patron saint of the parish.

The alternative venue for Mass was in people's homes. Word was put about locally that Mass would be said in a designated house on a selected day. The neighbours would gather for what was often the only opportunity to be at Mass for a long time. Because it was not safe for the priest to carry sacred vessels or vestments with him on his journeys, these were taken care of by the local people. They passed the "Mass kit" from house to house as it was needed.

This Mass became known as the "station Mass" because of the random movement from place to place. In some areas, some houses became known locally as regular venues for Mass and became known as Mass houses. More of these emerged as the Penal Laws were repealed but the Catholic community still did not have resources to build enough churches. Gradually, during the first half of the 19th century, churches were built across the countryside to replace the Mass houses.

During the years of the penal laws, it was in this ravine in Derrybeg where St Marys would one day stand, that Gweedore Catholics gathered into worship. When the laws were relaxed, and the people of Gweedore sought to build a permanent place of worship. This barren land was the only place they were allowed to use by the landlords of the time, who were reluctant to allow a Roman Catholic chapel on their land.

So, St Marys was built in the ravine above the river that would so dramatically overflow on that dreadful day 15Th of August 1880. Tragically five parishioners died with hundreds injured. The Irish Times labelled it as "The Gweedore Catastrophe" and the flood made headlines across the globe.

This is an account of the tragedy which appeared in the New Zealand Tablet on the 15th of October 1880.

Sir, — There comes to-day the sad news that on Sunday last, in a wild and romantic glen in Donegal, a mountain flood, bursting into the Catholic chapel during Divine Service, submerged the crowded building, several of the worshippers being swept away and drowned. I know the place well; and the singular circumstances and the curious history of the little church thus destroyed, while they explain the tragedy which has just occurred, afford us an illustrative glimpse of Ireland a hundred year ago. Between the pass of Dunlewy and the sea, about two miles from Lord George Hill's pretty rustic hotel at Gweedore, the traveller reaches the hamlet of Derrybeg.

Half a mile or more " up the glen" stands, or stood, the chapel in question. Even when told I was within a few perches of the edifice, I looked for it in vain on my first visit to the spot some years ago. After a while I noticed, rising, as it seemed in a brake of heather, a stone cross. Drawing nearer, I saw that the cross stood on the pointed gable of a building, the roof of which was below the level of the land around. I found myself on the brink of a wild ravine, at the narrow bottom of which a noisy mountain river brawled and danced its way from lake to sea. Down below, built across or upon the stream was the "chapel " of Derrybeg. Its walls on either hand almost touched the side of the rocky fissure, on which wild evergreens and dwarf oak clustered beautifully. I descended and found as neat and as impressive a little church as ever I entered, albeit everything was simplicity itself. All was well ordered; and scrupulous cleanliness and devotional care were observable in the most minute arrangements. Far remote as it was from the noisy world, I noted that even here the village blacksmith could bear his daughter's voice "singing in the village choir," for the hymn books and even the harmonium were at hand; while the river outside, and beneath the floor where I stood supplied a never-ending "thorough bass." Of course, I asked why so singular a spot had been chosen as the site of the building. "It was not all choice," replied my companion, the pastor of the district; " not an inch of ground would the neighbouring lords of the soil give us on which to erect a roof; we are here by proscription; " and then he told me the story. For nearly 200 years, or ever since the early part of the reign of Anne, this ravine was the secret place of worship for the Catholic peasantry of the neighbouring glens. Sentries were posted on the edge of the cliffs above, while, on either brink of the river below, the mountaineers knelt — a ledge on the rocks, still pointed out, sufficing as an altar. Indeed, the place afforded unusual advantages or facilities for such proscribed devotions, so easily could several hundreds of worshippers be secreted there. About 100 years ago the sentries happily were dispensed with, and a little wooden box was fixed on the natural altar ledge, so that the candles were not blown out by the wind. Later, a permanent wooden hut, open at the end facing down the river, was put up, within which the officiating priest and his attendant had room to stand or kneel. There are old men living near Dunlewy, I believe, who remember this hut — the river gorge, with the sky for a canopy, being the only church or chapel where the people prayed, under summer sun and winter rain, till a comparatively recent period. lam not astonished that, independently of the refusal of landlords to give a site for " a Popish chapel," this spot, hallowed by such memories and associations, should have been clung to by the people. So, thirty or forty years ago, they, by volunteer labour, blasted away the bottom rocks, bridged over the stream, and built their 'new chapel " in the cleft of the ravine I have described. I would ask you, sir, for kind permission to add a word or two about the poor people on whom the calamity of last Sunday has fallen— the congregation of worshippers in that little church. It is my belief that there does not breathe within our islands a rustic community more nearly approaching in simplicity of manners and purity of lives the picture Longfellow has drawn for us of life in the village of Grand Pre. Though privations have tried them sorely during the past year, they have contributed naught to the records* of disorder or crime. Death, swift and terrible, has now filled with wailing and grief their humble homes — these homes where, as I well know, a wayfarer ever found a smiling welcome, and wherein 'a stranger was a sacred name." Their good friend and benefactor, Mr. William A. Ross, of Dunlewy Castle, is now away in Egypt and may not hear of this tragedy for weeks to come. In his absence I shall be glad to receive and forward to the clergyman of the district, or to the Most Rev. Dr. Logue, the estimable Bishop of Raphoe, any help which kindly and sympathetic hearts on this side of the Channel may feel disposed to contribute. Iam aware, sir, that it is not lightly you permit any such appeal to the readers of the Times, and I can only hope that you may perceive in the circumstances of the case some ground for extending the privilege on the present occasion.

Yours very truly, A. M. Sullivan.(1)

Not only did the freak storm damage the Church but the surrounding countryside was devastated, houses rendered uninhabitable, livestock killed, and crops ruined. An appeal was sent to the British parliament for aid.

£100 was sent on the 18th of August as an initial amount with several members of the government contributing.

Father McFadden who became parish priest in 1875 continued to serve in the parish until 1901 during which time he challenged landlords for their cruel treatment of tenants and sought international aid for people who had been evicted from their homes.

The original St Mary's closed in the early 1970's with the opening of a new chapel on higher ground close-by. A memorial stands on the grounds of the old chapel in honour of those who perished in the flood. A mass is offered every year for those that died as Gweedore will never forget the great flood of 1880.

*Sources:*

1. *New ZEALAND Tablet, October 15, 1880*

# CHAPTER 17
# JAMES DUFFY WINNER OF THE VICTORIA CROSS

When the world was thrown into the carnage that would become known as WW1, In August 1914, there were already 25,000 Irishmen serving in the

British Army with another 30,000 in the army reserve.

However, by the end of the war in 1918, 200,000 Irishmen were involved in the conflict. This participation of Irishmen was proportionately the greatest deployment of armed manpower in the history of Irish militarism.

Sadly nearly 30,000 died serving in Irish regiments of the British forces, and about 49,400 died altogether, 1,200 of them from Donegal.

Men from Donegal fought on land, in the air and on ships around the globe not only in France but in Egypt, Mesopotamia and Palestine.

When war broke out no one could contemplate the

slaughter that would unfold as modern trench warfare replaced the massed cavalry charges and set piece open battles of the 19th century.

Nationalists, for whom the establishment of an Irish 'home rule' parliament in Dublin had been the principalpolitical aim for most of the 19th century, were committed to the war effort by their leader, John Redmond, in September 1914.

This was on the grounds that the necessary Home Rule legislation had been passed (though in fact it was suspended for the duration of the war), and that fight for the 'freedom of small nations' (such as Belgium or Serbia) was Ireland's fight as well. The plight of gallant, Catholic little Belgium, invaded by a militaristic aggressor, was disadvantageously compared with Ireland, achieving freedom (so Redmond argued) within the British Empire, rather like Canada or Australia.(1)

When German forces invaded Belgium a wave of patriotism swept the British empire including Ireland, with many believing the war to end all wars would be over by Christmas.

Sadly, this was not to be the case and as stalemate took hold in Europe, an insatiable demand for more and more men grew as the numbers of wounded and slaughtered increased.

All across Britain men were encouraged to enlist and Ireland was no different, in 1916, the Department of

Recruiting in Ireland wrote to Bishop O'Donnell, in Donegal, requesting: "that recruiting meetings might with advantage be held outside the Churches after Mass on Sundays and Holidays."(2)

Such was the rush to enlist that three new Army Divisions were quickly established the 10th (Irish), 16th (Irish) and the 36th (Ulster). Men from every parish and townland in Donegal helped swell the ranks.

Irishmen joined up for many reasons. Some were simply after adventure, like Tom Barry, later to become a noted IRA commander, who enlisted in June 1915 'to see what war was like, to get a gun, to see new countries and to feel like a grown man'.(3)

For others there was an economic motive. James Connolly, the socialist revolutionary, said that employment opportunities were so bad in Ireland that men had no choice but to enlist. It was, he asserted, 'economic conscription'.

No matter their reasons Donegal men joined established regiments such as the Royal Inniskilling Fusiliers, the Royal Irish Fusiliers, the Royal Irish Rifles, the Connaught Rangers, the Royal Munster Fusiliers, and the Royal Dublin Fusiliers.

Irishmen who had left home in search of work joined regiments in England, Scotland and Wales. Emigrants of the Diaspora enlisted in the armies of Australia, New Zealand, Canada, South Africa, India and the United

States. Some joined the Royal Flying Corps while others including many from Donegal were in the Royal Navy and became Merchant Seamen.

Recruitment however declined after 1916, Several factors contributed to this.

One was the heavy casualties suffered by Irish units in the war. The 10th Irish Division suffered terrible losses at Gallipoli in 1915, while the 16th and 36th Divisions were mired in the mud and suffered horrendous losses at the Battle of the Somme in 1916.

A second important factor was the Catholic Church's condemnation of the war in July 1915. Pope Benedict XV issued an encyclical calling on all powers to end the war and come to an agreement. As a result, the Irish Catholic Bishops publicly called on Redmond to withdraw Irish support for the war.

Thirdly, Irish troops in the British Army appear to have been treated with harshness even by the standards of the time. They constituted just two per cent of the membership of the force, yet they were the recipients of eight per cent (271) of all death sentences imposed by its courts-martials.

Opposition to the war in Ireland may have therefore been influenced by perceived discrimination by British High Command against Irish soldiers, although within the Irish unit's death sentences were meted out in roughly equal proportions against Catholic and Protestant servicemen.

On average one British soldier out of every 3,000 of their troops that died in the war did so due to being court martialled and executed by firing squad, compared to the much higher one out of every 600 of the Irish troops that died.

Out of the total that were executed, 26 have since been retroactively pardoned.

The fourth and in my view the most important reason was the rise of radical nationalism because of the Easter Rising of 1916. After the failed insurrection in Dublin left around 500 dead, many Irishmen now felt it was better to die for Ireland than an empire that was fast becoming a dangerous oppressor and enemy of self-determination. Despite the unrest in Ireland, the death toll on the continent continued to rise.

Among them were men from Gweedore, such as Daniel Boyle from Middle Dore, James O'Donnell from Ballindrait and Owen Harkin from Carrickastakin who all made the ultimate sacrifice.

One Gweedore man would go onto be awarded the highest level of gallantry available to a soldier serving in the British army, the Victoria cross awarded for valour "in the presence of the enemy".

Irishmen had been awarded the Victoria Cross since

its creation in January 1856 by Queen Victoria to honour acts of valour during the Crimean War.

30 Irish VCs were awarded in the Crimean War, 59 Irish VCs in the Indian Mutiny, 46 Irish VCs in numerous other British Empire campaigns between 1857 and 1914, 37 Irish VCs in World War I, and eight Irish VCs in World War II.

The Gweedore man who won his VC was James Duffy and this is his story.

James Duffy was born on the 17th of November 1889 in the home of his mother, Catherine Doogan, at Thorr, in the parish of Gaoth Dobhair.

His father was Peter Duffy and James was the third son of the couple.

Peter was working in Bonagee, Letterkenny, and the family joined him when James was just a few months old. James attended a local primary school in Drumlodge, near Letterkenny.

His father was employed on a seasonal basis in the agricultural and fishing industries, picking up work wherever and whenever he could. James would go on to try his hand at fishing but like so many of the young men in Ireland at that time it was not long before he crossed the water to Scotland to Glasgow. He quickly found work in the massive shipyards that lined the river Clyde working in the famous John Brown Shipyard in Clydebank.

When war broke out James was still working in the Shipyards but along with thousands of other young men he was swept up in the jingoistic fervour of the time he quickly enlisted. He did so on the 1st of December 1914, joining the 6th (Service) Battalion, Royal Inniskilling Fusiliers, which had been raised in Omagh, Co. Tyrone, in August.

The battalion was part of the 31st Brigade, 10th (Irish) Division, the first complete Irish division to serve with the Army. The constituent member regiments were drawn from Ireland's four provinces and it's early training took place in the Dublin area.

The Division moved to Basingstoke, Hampshire in May 1915 and was ear marked to participate in the ill-fated Gallipoli campaign which had stalled and descended into the static trench warfare that had blighted the western front.

In July Duffy and his regiment embarked for the Gallipoli Peninsula, arriving on Mudros on the 7th of August. The 10th (Irish) Division later landed on "C" Beach, south of Suvla Bay, and Duffy was soon busy as the battalion went into action.

While the landing was successful, heavy fighting continued throughout August as the Allies attempted to expand the beach head they had created and move inland. However, the offensive failed. During the summer months the hot conditions, and a constant struggle by the allies to supply enough fresh drinking water to its troops, meant that conditions at Gallipoli were awful. Large numbers of troops, on both sides, succumbed to a dysentery epidemic that spread across the peninsula in the late summer.

The cost of Gallipoli was enormous in terms of human life, with an estimated 130,000 men losing their life in action or from diseases contracted while on the peninsula. In that total are approximately 4,000 Irish men who never returned home.(4)

The 6th Royal Inniskilling's were later transferred to the Salonika front on the 24th of October and were involved in the fighting of the 7th and 8th December, at Kosturino and then Karajakois, and remained in the theatre of operations until September 1917, when they were posted to Alexandria, to prepare for the forthcoming invasion of Palestine.

On the 1st of November, the battalion captured Abu Irgeig, and took part in the successful operations in the Third Battle of Gaza when the British forces under the command of General Edmund Allenby successfully broke the Turkish defensive Gaza-Beersheba line. The critical moment of the battle was the capture of the town of Beersheba on the first day by Australian light horsemen.

Throughout his time in Palestine, Duffy was kept busy in his role as stretcher bearer and on the 27th of

December, he performed the following act which was to lead to the award of the VC.

> "While his company was holding an exposed position, Private Duffy (a stretcher bearer) and another stretcher-bearer went out to bring in a seriously wounded comrade; when the other stretcher-bearer was wounded, he returned to get another man, when again going forward the relief stretcher-bearer was killed.
>
> Private Duffy then went forward alone, and under heavy fire succeeded in getting both wounded men under cover and attended to their injuries. His gallantry undoubtedly saved both men's lives, and he showed throughout an utter disregard of danger under very heavy fire".(5)

Six months after the fighting in which Duffy performed his heroic deeds, the battalion were sent to France and landed at Marseilles on the 1st of June 1918.

James Duffy was presented with his Victoria Cross by the King George IV in the quadrangle of Buckingham Palace on the 25th of July 1918, and later returned home to Bonagee, where he was given a rousing reception.

Later that year, James married Maggie Hegarty, and the couple went on to have seven children and twenty-four grandchildren. Duffy was demobilised in 1919, little knowing that he was never to enjoy the luxury of regular employment again.

If he did find work it was usually as a casual labourer on the roads or on farms when the harvest was due in, but ill health and the situation in Ireland during the 1920's conspired against him, which included being kidnapped by the IRA in 1921, because he had served in the British Army and was of a higher profile than many others because of the VC.

It appears that Duffy missed out on several VC events, including the VC Garden Party of 1920 and the service for the Unknown Warrior, due to the non-arrival of the invitations which were incorrectly addressed. The matter was resolved in time for the 1929 House of Lords VC Dinner and Duffy attended the event.

In 1934, he took part in the 'Londonderry' Armistice Parade, but his ill health continued to cause problems for him, and he was living off a disability pension for malaria and rheumatism of 13 shillings and 6 pence a week, out of which he had to pay 2 shillings and 6 pence for the rent of his cottage in Bonagee.(6)

When he was ill, Duffy was sent to Leopardstown Hospital, Dublin, where he received a much-needed boost to his income with a weekly grant of 25 shillings from a fund set up by a wealthy American businessman for distressed VC recipients and the Royal British Legion assisted when they could.

Duffy's misery continued when his wife passed away in 1944, and it is reported that pressure from within the family to sell the VC to the highest bidder may have caused some friction, but Duffy bequeathed his medals, in the event of his death, to his former regiment in 1949.

In 1956, he attended the Dublin Festival of Remembrance, where he joined three other VC recipients, Sir Adrian Carton de Wiart VC, KBE, CB, CMG, DSO (1916), Joseph Woodhall VC (1918) and John Moyney VC (1917), and later the VC Centenary celebrations in London. Two years later he was invited to a dinner held in Dublin to commemorate the six Irish regiments that were disbanded in 1922.(7)

Duffy was, like many other VC recipients, reluctant to speak of his actions that led to the VC and would often play down the award, but the medal attracted attention and on at least one occasion Duffy was visited by Earl Mountbatten during one of his regular summer holidays to Ireland.

In 1966 James Duffy met the Queen when she attended the 50th anniversary of the Battle of the Somme at the Balmoral Showgrounds, Belfast.

On the 7th of April 1969, following a long illness, Duffy passed away at Drumany, Co. Donegal, and was buried in Conwal Cemetery, Letterkenny, Co. Donegal.

He was afforded a full military funeral which was arranged by Major George Shields, Chairman of the

Belfast branch of the Royal Inniskilling Fusiliers Regimental Association, and who had served with Duffy in 1917, and by Archdeacon Louis Crooks, who had become a good friend of Duffy's. The funeral began at Duffy's cottage and his coffin had to be passed through the sitting room window and was carried by eight members of the Royal Irish Rangers, led by CSM William O'Neill and the cortege was led by Piper Major James Creggan who played the lament "Flowers of the Forest".(8)

A Requiem Mass was held at St. Eunan's Cathedral in Letterkenny, and then moved onto the cemetery passing through the town.

The shops and offices closed, lorries, cars and buses were parked up on the side of the road and their drivers stood along with the majority of the population in silence as the cortege passed, and it was reported that the only sound to be heard was the clink of the medals of the old soldiers.

Duffy was laid to rest beside his wife and several wreaths were laid before Lance-Corporal J. Maxwell, played The Last Post and then Reveille at the graveside. Duffy left five sons and one daughter and in 1997, one of the sons, Hugh, was buried with his parents. Ten years later a stone bench was unveiled in Letterkenny Town Park on the 10th of July 2007 to honour Duffy.

His daughter Nellie was present when former

Letterkenny Mayor Ciaran Brogan unveiled the bench in one of his final duties in the office.(9)

Private Duffy was again honoured when Chaplain to the Irish army's Finner Camp, Bundoran, Fr Alan Ward celebrated a Mass in his memory at Donegal County Museum. Private Duffy's Victoria Cross was brought from the Inniskilling Museum for the service.

In November 2017, the Ulster History Circle unveiled a blue plaque at Castle Street, Letterkenny in his honour. (10) I can't but think that perhaps as the passing years have healed old wounds, the time has come for some memorial to James in his native townland of Gweedore.

*Sources:*

1. *Professor Keith Jeffery, March 2011*

2. *http://www.irelandsgreatwar.ie/*

3. *Guerrilla Days in Ireland, Tom Barry*

4. *London Gazette, February 26, 1918*

5. *www.history.com*

6. *vconline.org.uk*

7. *vconline.org.uk*

8. *vconline.org.uk*

9. *Donegal News, July 2007*

10. *Donegal Democrat, November 2017*

# CHAPTER 18

# LET THERE BE LIGHT—
# ELECTRIFICATION OF
# GWEEDORE

**D**aily life in rural Ireland before the onset of electrification was best described as a constant struggle just to complete the mundane tasks that we all take for granted today.

Farm work had to be done by hand and in daylight. Any water required had to be drawn from a well. Most homes cooked every meal on an open fire and food could not be refrigerated. Clothes had to be washed by hand and the washing and toilet facilities were primitive to say the least.

## THE EARLY DAYS OF ELECTRICITY IN IRELAND

Thomas Edison produced the first reliable and commercially usable electric light bulb in 1879 and the history of electricity in Ireland began soon after in 1880, when the first public electric light was installed at Princes Street in Dublin at the Freeman's Journal offices.

In the same year, the Dublin electrical service venders and the municipal council created the Dublin electric light company to provide public street lighting.

By 1882, the Dublin Electric Light Company operated three coal-fired generation stations in the city at Fade Street, Schoolhouse Lane and Liffey Street.(1)

In 1884, there was a proposal that the lower Shannon area should become the industrial hub of Ireland. The River Shannon had long been the focus of various plans to bring electricity to Ireland.

Early iterations of the project were deemed unfeasible and were delayed by political unrest in Ireland and by the outbreak of World War I.

Dublin Corporation constructed a coal-fired power station at the Pigeon House in Ringsend in 1904 using imported coal as fuel.

## A BRIGHT VISION FOR THE FUTURE

In 1923, a young engineer from Drogheda called Thomas McLaughlin returned to Ireland after a period working abroad with Siemens in Berlin and studying hydroelectric schemes throughout Europe. With this knowledge, he proposed damming the River Shannon and building an electric power station at Ardnacrusha in County Clare to bring power to towns and cities all around Ireland.

During his time in Germany, McLaughlin concluded that peat or coal were not a viable solution to Ireland's future energy needs, and together with his colleagues in Siemens, he suggested that hydro-electric power was a more realistic option for utilising the native resources available in the fledgling Irish Free State.(2)

In 1925, in collaboration with the Siemens company and Patrick McGilligan TD, the minister for Industry and Commerce, McLaughlin succeeded in getting a 'White Paper' on the scheme accepted by the Irish government. A budget of £5.1 million was allocated to the ambitious project – 20% of Ireland's national revenue for that time. A bill labelled the "Shannon Water and Electricity Power Act", that proposed the diversion of water from the Shannon to a canal in Doonas was passed in 1925 and work began on the Shannon Scheme in August of that year.

Siemens was handed the contract and the project involved work at two major locations in County Clare, at a generating station at Ardnacrusha and a weir at Parteen.

During construction, 4,000 Irish and 1,000 Germans worked and lived on-site.

An overarching body was required to take electricity forward in Ireland. This was because the Irish electricity service was totally fragmented with more than 300 different suppliers concerned with generating and supplying electricity in various parts of the country, including 16 local authorities and five major private companies.

While several options for the management of the new Shannon Scheme were considered, McLaughlin, passionately believed that rapid progress could only be achieved through unified control of production and distribution. This approach provided the impetus for the passing of the Electricity Supply Act in 1927, which created the Electricity Supply Board (ESB), the first semi-state body in Ireland, and with McLaughlin as its first Managing Director.(3)

## SHANNON COMES ONLINE

In July 1929, the Shannon scheme was completed and officially opened by Taoiseach W T Cosgrove. It was generating electricity in October of the same year. By 1935 it was producing 80 per cent of Ireland's electricity.

The scale of the project and the vision of its sponsors should not be underestimated and at the time, it was the largest hydroelectric station in the world, though this was soon superseded by the Hoover Dam, which commenced construction in 1930.

The Financial times was also impressed with the completed project saying:

> "They have thrown on their shoulders the not easy task of breaking what is in reality an enormous inferiority complex and the Shannon Scheme is one - and probably the most vital - of their methods of doing it".(4)

Electricity from the Shannon Scheme was supplied to roughly 240,000 premises in towns and cities only, leaving over 400,000 rural dwellings without power.

New hydroelectric plants were commissioned, and peat was considered as an alternative fuel source for electricity generation in parallel with the goal of rural electrification policies.

However, the financial resources were not available to extend electricity to rural Ireland in the 1920s and 1930s.

As the 30s drew to an end, the ESB and The Irish government began working on broad plans for rural electrification, and the state agreed to subsidise its roll out. However, the outbreak of World War II in 1939 delayed the process.

With coal rationed, peat was promoted as a viable alternative; one that included the benefits of being indigenous, widely available and, from a socio-economic point of view, advantageous to rural Ireland.

## THE CASE FOR RURAL ELECTRIFICATION

Work did not start on rural electrification until the end of World War II or as it was called in Ireland the 'Emergency'.

It was not until the Rural Electrification Scheme (1946) and the Electricity Supply Amendment Act (1955) were passed that the electricity network started to reach the most rural and isolated communities in the country.

Dr Thomas McLaughlin, the driving force behind the Shannon project and now the Managing Director of the ESB believed that rural electrification represented: "the application of modern science and engineering to raise the standard of rural living and to get to the root of the social evil of the "flight from the land".(5)

The task that faced the ESB was herculean, a suitable modern-day comparison would be the challenge the state has in installing rural broadband. Thankfully in the ESB the state had an organisation with men and women up to the task.

The State was divided into 792 areas – roughly along parish boundaries. This was a clever strategy as the ESB recruited at least one local influencer in each area who could encourage their friends and neighbours to sign up to get connected to the new network.

Rural electrification began in earnest when the first pole in phase one was raised on November 5th, 1946, at Kilsallaghan, in north Co Dublin. The first lights of the scheme were switched on at Oldtown, Co Dublin, in January 1947.(6)

## PROMOTING ELECTRICITY TO RURAL IRELAND

One of the most potent propaganda tools in rural Ireland at the time was the parish priest in the pulpit. Throughout rural Ireland the ESB worked with the local clergy, who were then used to extoll the virtues of the new technology and the benefits of electrification.

Although it would never be economically viable to connect some sparsely populated areas the strategy was simple, the more people who wanted a connection the sooner their area would be visited and worked upon.

The approach in every district was the same. The ESB asked householders if they wanted to sign up for electricity, then held local information meetings.

In the first long phase of electrification, which ran from 1946 to 1965, it was sometimes your hard luck if you wanted to be connected but your nearest neighbours did not.

This was because the ESB deemed it uneconomic to run lines to just one house. The areas with the highest take-up were first to be connected.

Although some people did not want change, and others worried about whether the wires might set their thatch roofs on fire, most people who refused connection did so for financial reasons.

That "uneconomic acceptance" was a category on the forms which showed how widespread rural poverty was. The scheme was heavily subsidised, but, depending on the size of the premises, householders had to pay a connection fee, along with future bills, and to wire their homes before they were connected.

The people who first agreed to sign up but then changed their minds were called 'backsliders'.

In May 1954, in Ballivor, Co Meath, 290 people said they wanted electricity. Nineteen changed their minds, for reasons that are stark examples of poverty in 1950s rural Ireland such as: "No funds. House semi-derelict." "Refused supply due to lack of funds." "Has large family and could not pay fixed charge." "Both labourers out of work." "Recently widowed. No funds."(7)

Throughout the length and breadth of Ireland politicians of all political shades lobbied the ESB for their area to be electrified. It wasn't just politicians who tried to exert their influence

In July 1957, the parish priest of Ballycroy county Mayo wrote to the Rural Electrification Office. He said that his parishioners were anxious and that they believed he could influence decisions at the Dublin head office. "Sometimes people get an idea that the PP isn't taking any interest in these matters. I need not add that I have a very deep interest in the light coming to Ballycroy."(8)

Sadly, his appeal fell on deaf ears, due to economics and it wasn't until April 1964 before electricity at last came to the parish.

## A HERCULEAN EFFORT

The Rural Electric Scheme was a massive project, the work would require more than one million poles erected with 78,754km of wire used. It would eventually cost £36M equivalent to €1.5BN today.

The first phase of the scheme ended in 1965 and by then, over 300,000 homes were connected.

Post-development plans and extensions ran until 1978 when Blackvalley, Co Kerry received electricity. By 1975, 99% of Irish homes were connected to the same electricity grid.

The Rural Electrification Scheme employed up to 40 separate units of 50-100 workers, spread across 26,000 square miles. Many of these units were stationed in remote localities, and daily face-to-face communication was impossible.(9)

Such a widely dispersed workforce presented the Rural Electrification Office (REO) with a challenge – how could it ensure fast and efficient communication among its staff?

The solution was suggested by the chief engineer in charge of the project William Roe who quickly recognised the vital importance of good communication across the nation to ensure the success of the scheme. He told the ESB:

> "If a high standard of performance was to be achieved, the staff needed not alone to be well briefed and motivated from the start, but to be constantly refreshed with information on the progress of the scheme, advised of developments in all aspects of the work, sustained when difficulties arose and motivated to give of their best at all times".(10)

Roes' solution was simple but innovative for the time he created a magazine for employees called REO news.

In December 1947, the first edition informed all those working on the scheme that: "In order to keep the rural staff informed of the progress of the rural Electrification scheme it is intended to issue REO news monthly".(11)

It covered a variety of topics, including personnel and transfers of staff; the delivery and distribution of materials; sales figures and league tables; area notes; engineer and progress reports; news items and articles of interest; as well as sports and social pages, letters to the editor, and photographs.

A focus on progress, staff league tables and sales figures all succeeded in instilling a sense of rivalry among the workers, inspiring them towards greater effort.

There were 168 issues of REO News published between December 1947 and November 1961, growing from three to over 20 pages. In 1953, the magazine was given a glossy cover, and included a number of black and white photographs, and by 1959, REO News was published in a fully printed format. From 1948, REO News also printed a special December issue.(12)

## ELECTRICITY COMES TO GWEEDORE.

The rural electrification program finally reached Gweedore in August 1955 and by the time it ended over a year later, 370 homes had been connected and 1,155 poles erected on a line that stretched 108 kilometres across bog land, hill and glen.

Reports at the time complained of what was termed serious backsliding in Gweedore. This was when someone initially asked for their home to be connected to the grid but then declined the service. This was mostly due to economic pressures rather than a fear of new technology.

A report from September 1955 states:

"At the time of writing his report Mr Kerr had not final costs but anticipates that there will be a considerable amount of over expenditure. Backsliding was fairly serious at a total of 74, but 128 new consumers created a net increase in revenue of approximately £570.

Agriculture is practically non-existent in the area, and accordingly, sales of domestic equipment to the value of £950 by the A.O., Mr P Dawson, must be regarded as reasonably satisfactory".(13)

However, electricity was soon almost universal and in 1959 the REO reported a story that highlighted the changes in rural Gweedore:

"During the mobile Farm Kitchen's stay in Gweedore, Co. Donegal, it was reported in February 1959 REO news how the Bakewell Oven was delivered by sleigh in the snow to a gas consumer for trial. For your information, the gas consumer has since got rid of her gas cooker and installed a 3-PLAte electric cooker complete with automatic time control. And by all accounts the whole house is delighted with the change".(14)

The story of electrification continued 50 years after the homes of Gweedore were switched on when on the 26th of August 2005 Gola Island was finally connected to the national grid and the mains water supply.

## THE GWEEDORE TURF BURNING STATION

After the end of the 'Emergency' – or World War II for those of you outside Ireland – the Irish Government decided to begin a large-scale development of one of their natural resources the wild peat bogs of Ireland to be overseen by Bord na Móna. Part of this exercise was to be the building of turf burning stations across Ireland. This would not only provide much needed local employment but help bring electricity to rural Ireland. Work began on the first four stations in the west of Ireland Scríb, Co. Galway, Miltown Malbay in Co. Clare, Cahersiveen in Co. Kerry and Gweedore in Co. Donegal. These would eventually cost £500,000 each.

Work began in Gweedore in 1954 on the picturesque banks of Loch Mhín na Cuinge. and the station was commissioned in 1958.

When the construction of Gweedore and Clady stations was in progress, the metering for supply to the site was mounted at the roadside, on a pole. The meter reader for the area dutifully recorded the readings on his rounds and made his returns in the regulation manner.

Of course, the meter on the pole was purely for records purposes, and it must have been a puzzled Site Clerk who found in the post one morning a notification that if the E.S.B. bill wasn't paid in seven days, the supply would be cut off!

Gweedore has always been noted for its efficiency. Built in one of the most spectacular locations in Ireland the Gweedore turf Burning station was a huge, green, steel building, it soared incongruously out of the rugged landscape of north-west Donegal. Standing on the banks of Loch Mhín na Cuinge at the foot of the majestic peak of Errigal the highest mountain in Donegal it was surrounded by the beauty of the wild western Donegal.

The ESB began operating the power station in 1958. The energy it generated was initially fed into the Donegal loop and subsequently into the national grid. Hand-cut turf was taken from 200 local suppliers who lived within a 20-mile radius. The turf was hauled there initially by cart and later by tractor.

Gweedore station stood like a monument to the achievement of the local people who played a major part in the station's operation. Two miles away, at the mouth of the lake, the Clady River was diverted to form the head race for the remote-control hydro station.

The two stations, Clady and Gweedore, supplied a total of 9MW to the Irish electricity network. Negligible, you might think; but the change in the economic conditions in the locality was sufficient to justify the cost of building and running these remote stations, without any reference to their efficiency, which, by all reports was beyond reproach.

Around 30,000 tons of turf was burned annually when the station was at its peak. This was a much-needed source of additional income for subsistence farmers in the area of not just Gweedore but the Rosses and Cloughaneely.

When operations began it was at first not easy to get supplies of sufficient quantity and quality to meet the stations requirements.

As the station grew however the ESB had to administer a quota system among the 380 contractors.

While most of the turf supplied was of a decent standard the quality of some was questionable.

One man's job was to go around and inspect the clamps of turf on the bogs supplying the station, to ensure that it was dry enough before it was brought to the station by lorry.

If the turf arriving at the station was too wet, it had to

be rejected, as it would not burn efficiently in the furnaces.

One former employee recorded in the 70s that:

"The turf would be tipped into a big hopper, then carried off into a grate which was eight or nine feet wide, to be burned. The heat produced converted the water supplied by the local lake into steam and this was used to drive the turbines "fire eats steel" and he can remember how at one stage the chimney on the power station had to be replaced as it wasn't lagged to protect it from the surging heat. "The station provided much-needed employment for the local area," he added. "Although it was never viable, never made a profit, the ESB kept it going."(15)

With a minimal level of electrical output and running at a constant financial loss why was the Turf Burning station built and then kept open in Gweedore?

The first reason was to support the rural electrification exercise which had begun in Gweedore in August 1954 and had finished in July 1955.

The second was to obviously boost the local economy in a deprived area of Ireland more used to emigration rather than indigenous industry.

Gweedore and the surrounding parishes had been used to its menfolk leaving the parish from St Patricks day until Christmas to toil in the tattie fields of Scotland or to work in the building sites of the UK. Many would never return permanently and instead raise their families in Irish enclaves of London, Liverpool and Glasgow.

Supplying the turf burning station gave an income that allowed some to stay at home.

The rise in the standard of living for some was evident in the number of homes who owned a car or in whose kitchens people would gather to watch the evolving RTE on television.

## THE END OF THE TURF STATION

However, the Turf station would never make a profit and it was finally closed in 1996.

Despite locals pleading to use the building for a cultural centre it was finally demolished in 2002.

The Clady Hydro Electric plant is however still in operation.

So ended the Turf burning station that had so helped the electrification of Gweedore and the surrounding parishes and who brought light to Gweedore.

## LIFE AFTER THE SWITCH ON

Once a community was connected, or about to be connected, the ESB held public demonstrations of household appliances. These were then sold bringing electric irons, kettles, stoves to homes.

When electricity came to rural Ireland the lives of many were transformed and life changed suddenly, from having to go to the shop to buy paraffin to being able to turn on the light at the flick of a switch.

Small towns and rural townlands became brighter and winters less harsh and Christmas more special as the fairy lights began to shine. It also gave rise to a rural Irish icon as every house had the Sacred Heart picture with the red lamp, many didn't get a kettle and washing machine until later on.

While it may have made life easier it also had a deep cultural impact on rural Ireland.

The roll out of electricity allowed the growth of mass communication mediums such as cinema, radio and eventually television. These had massive influence spreading cultural norms from abroad especially America and the United Kingdom.

Despite the power of Catholic church, these influences began to change rural Ireland as young people began to absorb the new cultural messages and trends and took advantage of the new opportunities offered by the new technology.

However cultural historians have also argued that the rural electrification process rather than diluting the native Gaelic Irish culture actually played an important part in saving the Irish language.

> "It must not be forgotten that native culture used the new media to diffuse itself too. Gaelic sports, Irish music and even the Irish language gained a second life. Arguably the Irish language may well have become virtually dead but for its adaptation in radio, the newsreel, television and now through information technology".(16)

When you consider the scale of the project that the ESB undertook with rural electrification and the changes it made to so many lives, the people of Ireland owe a debt of gratitude to the visionaries like Thomas McLaughlin and the many men who raised the million poles that finally brought power to the homes and farms of rural Ireland and Gweedore.

**Sources:**

1. *Ireland2050.ie*
2. *ESB Archives, 2016*
3. *ESB Archives, 2016*
4. *Financial Times, July 1927*
5. *ESB Archives, 2016*
6. *ESB Archives, 2016*

7. *Irish Times, October 29, 2016*

8. *Irish Times, October 29, 2016*

9. *ESB Archives, 2016 10 ESB Archives, 2016*

10. *ESB Archives, 2016*

11. *REO News, September 1955*

12. *REO News, August 1959*

13. *ESB Archives, 2016*

14. *ESB Archives, 2016*

15. *Dr Séamas Mac Philib, www.ouririshheritage.org*

# ALSO BY THE AUTHOR

If you enjoyed *Famine, Murder and Eviction,* then
why not check out John Joe's other books.

### THE IRISH WISE GUYS

*The Irish Wise Guys* tells the story
of Americas most notorious Irish-
American gangsters.

Men who rose from poverty to
control criminal empires and who
made millions, and then more often
than not met a violent end.

### THE IRISH IN POWER

*The Irish In Power* is for anyone
interested in Irish-American politics.

It looks at the Irish men and
women elected to office in their new
home, who created history while
helping forge a superpower.

Both available from *glassaghpublishing.ie* and *Amazon in
paperback and Kindle*

Printed in Great Britain
by Amazon

19925533R00169